Strange Ghosts

Strange Ghosts

essays by Darren Greer

Cormorant Books

THE CANADA COUNCIL | LE CONSEIL DES ARTS
FOR THE ARTS | DU CANADA
SINCE 1957 | DEPUIS 1957

ONTARIO ARTS COUNCIL
CONSEIL DES ARTS DE L'ONTARIO

The publisher gratefully acknowledges the support of the
Canada Council for the Arts and the Ontario Arts Council
for its publishing program. We acknowledge the financial support
of the Government of Canada through the Book Publishing
Industry Development Program (BPIDP) for our publishing activities.

Printed and bound in Canada

LIBRARY AND ARCHIVES CANADA CATALOGUING IN PUBLICATION

Greer, Darren
Strange ghosts: essays/Darren Greer. — 1st ed.

ISBN 1-896951-63-5

1. Greer, Darren. 2. Authors, Canadian (English) — 21st century — Biography.
I. Title.

PS8563.R4315Z47 2006   C814'.6   C2003-907282-7

Cover design: Derek von Essen
Text design: Tannice Goddard/Soul Oasis Networking
Cover image: Derek von Essen
Author Photo: Barry McConnell
Printer: Canadian Printco Limited

CORMORANT BOOKS INC.
215 SPADINA AVENUE, STUDIO 230, TORONTO, ON CANADA M5T 2C7
www.cormorantbooks.com

For my father

CONTENTS

REMEMBERING
FELIX PARTZ

I

In 1995 I checked into a drug and
alcohol treatment centre in Ottawa, where I stayed under super-
vision and in therapy for eleven months while I rid myself of a
nasty and progressively worsening cocaine habit. The treatment
centre sits in a busy downtown market, not far from the National
Gallery of Canada. On Sundays some of us would go there, because
we were bored, because it was free, and because it was something
to do on a day when there was no group therapy and we were
going crazy thinking about getting stoned. When I look back on it,
it makes me smile: there we were, a gang of long-haired, rough-
necked addicts, some of whom had been in prison a good portion
of their adult lives, roaming the hushed and hallowed halls of the
gallery. We chose the contemporary art rooms, which we found
more entertaining than the portraiture, realist, and religious art
of previous centuries. We preferred the iconoclastic, if obscure,
geometric paintings of Piet Mondrian, the neon installations of
Dan Flavin, the crazily elongated and rough-hewn sculpture of the
brothers Giocometti, to yet another painting of Christ on the cross

or as a baby in his mother's arms. We laughed at some of the stuff we saw, scoffed at others, and rarely admitted to liking anything. In those early days of treatment — with insides still raw and unsophisticated, as colourfully and emotionally charged as the canvases of the late abstract expressionist Mark Rothko — we were careful not to say anything that might expose us to ridicule.

And yet, over the course of those days and months, my appreciation for modern art began to be shaped. It was not, at first, any one piece that influenced me. It was rather the experience of twentieth-century art as a whole. After wandering through the other halls of sculpture and painting — 500 years of work that looked and felt the same, and replicated itself century after century with what seems from this modern perspective as the tiniest of innovations — coming into the contemporary-art rooms was like stepping into an alien world. The art of all the previous centuries looked like it was created not just in a different time period, but by a whole different species. I'm sure an art historian could draw the links between a Canaletto and a Mondrian, but I certainly could not. To me, what happened in the twentieth-century world of art was an explosion of form and idea and colour and content — a radical and frightening change from all that had gone before.

I began to go back to the gallery and to wander through the rooms of contemporary art by myself. I began also to catalogue, to decide what I liked and what I didn't — to understand that art is not always purely representative. More important than the space it occupies on the wall and floor is its positions in the imagination. Dan Flavin's neon creations are as much a comment on technology and industrialization as they are the deliberate manipulation of the haunting beauty of incandescent light. Piet

Mondrian reduced his subjects to coloured boxes and geometric squares precisely because everything *can* be so regulated.

But the true revelation came, as it often will, from something entirely unexpected and unrelated. Seventy-two days into my treatment program I was diagnosed HIV-positive. This was a staggeringly difficult thing for me to deal with. I waffled between leaving the centre, committing suicide, and going home to Nova Scotia to die, since I believed my death would be imminent.

On the first morning after my diagnosis I awoke in my dorm bed at dawn, and heard birds singing in a tree outside my window. I had awoken in that room for seventy-two days in a row, sometimes depressed, often confused, never once understanding how I had transformed from a young man with talent and promise to this — a twenty-seven-year-old drug addict with no prospect for a future and an unwillingness to glance back at a painful and often delinquent past living at a Salvation Army hostel. In those seventy-two days of treatment purgatory, I honestly could not recall having heard birds singing outside my window before, and, after lying in bed for an hour listening to them and thinking hard about my life, I decided to take it as a sign.

I chose to stay in treatment, despite the HIV diagnosis. A few weeks later I found myself, on a Sunday afternoon, in the National Gallery of Canada once again, looking at one particular exhibit. That was the year Felix Partz and the Canadian art-making team General Idea placed three gigantic AZT capsules on the floor of one room of the gallery. On the walls of the room were glued smaller replicas of the capsules — they were about the size of footballs, dissected and arranged in the pattern of days in the month on a calendrical page — one page of capsules for each month of the year. There had been some public furor about the cost of this exhibit. I agreed the first time I saw it. I might have been gay, but I didn't think much about AIDS then. Half a million dollars for this? This time, however, things were different. My doctor had started me on a regimen of AZT. I stood in the middle of that room of giant capsules and cried. I got it. Boy, did I get it. Modern art had spoken to me, in an awfully narrow, shared band of experience 4 | — not one that everyone would want to share. But I understood emotionally then what I understand intellectually now: the so-called twentieth-century collapse of the relationship between art and society had not been a collapse at all. Like so much in that turbulent century, it had been both a fracturing and a narrowing of our shared bands of common experience, which brought with it the loss of universal ideals and universal appeal. It seemed to me that *all* my understanding — not just of art, but of politics and religion and, especially, my relationship to myself — changed forever on that day. All because of a few guys; some plastic moulds, chicken wire and paints; and a desperate desire to communicate an idea, even if only a few people would really understand it, or would really want to.

II

I realize now it was this work by General Idea and those early visits to the Ottawa gallery that planted the seeds for my novel *Still Life with June*. The process of gathering material to write novels is not a conscious one. I never thought, *I'll write a book about this someday*. In fact, shortly after that I started a novel about something else entirely. But six years later I began *June*, a story about a man who works at a Salvation Army treatment centre and visits an art gallery on his days off and falls in love with one particular and obscure piece of modern art. I began the book one evening when I was restless, when I was almost sick from the desire to write, but I had no idea what I wanted to write about. I was suffering from a form of writer's block — an inability to move forward because I didn't know where I wanted to go. These blank spaces in between creative writing projects have always been very frightening for me. I want to write; I need to write, but I can't. I've been through this a few times now, and I should be able to convince myself that it will come with time. But the gut, where all good writing comes from, has no memory or logic. It lives entirely in the present. Each non-productive period will last forever, it tells me. Each block will be permanent. Each novel will be the last.

Yet somehow, during all this, *June* was begun. I wrote through the first draft in six weeks, and almost from the first I knew it was a different book for me. Like the modern art I had been influenced by, it flouted conventional forms. Some chapters were short — no more than a few paragraphs, and sometimes just a few words. Other chapters were simply lists made by the narrator, or positional statements, or e-mails. For those six weeks I barely slept or ate. My place became a mess and my cats were seriously neglected. Friends knocked on my door with dinner plans, only to be turned away. And yet, in the end, I was satisfied: I knew that something of my experience during those months in treatment had been caught; I felt I had created characters that were interesting, alive, and vibrant. They were very, very modern.

The road to publishing *June* was fairly bumpy. My first readers loved it — most large publishers in Canada admired it but didn't quite get it. One editor called it "too relentlessly first-person." Given that the novel plays with the idea of first-person narrative, I could both understand this and dismiss it at the same time. Another said she worked with writers all day, and so didn't feel like editing a book about one. I couldn't help wondering if many of the other types of characters in the book — Down's syndrome patients, convicted criminals, Salvation Army officers, concert pianists, and drug addicts — were roaming the halls of her publishing house, and was she sick of those too? But, by and large, I wasn't worried. I knew *June* would be published, and if she could get unscathed past the strained, often myopic perceptions of editors, people would like her. More importantly, I liked her, and still do. It seemed to me, while writing that novel, that what had happened with visual art had no near equivalent in writing — the doors of nineteenth-century convention had yet to be blown off in the latter the way they had been in the former. They had been refitted, certainly, by the likes of Eliot and Pound, Jeffers and Pynchon. Samuel Beckett and James Joyce had even kicked them in a few times. But the truth was the doors of modern literature were still hanging off the same old barn. In visual art, the barn has been burned and the entire structure has been replaced several times.

In some ways, this is understandable. The risk with trying stylistically radical prose is that the work will become focussed on form at the expense of content. Indeed, as many modern visual artists know, this is precisely the complaint people make about modern art: it is all idea, without any attempt at basic human communication. And who am I to say that some of it isn't guilty of this? A good portion of what passes for modern art is so subjective that it doesn't mean anything except to the artist; or the actual objective meaning is buried so deeply in the intellectual that the work doesn't engage the memory or the emotions, two of the pillars upon which the human imagination rests. Given that literature is so reliant on emotion and memory, fiction writers have always been a little afraid to experiment too grandly with form for fear of alienating their audience, or even alienating themselves from their own characters. Certainly this is why I never strayed far from the lyrical, the realistic, the straight forwardly descriptive. Until *June*, that is. I make no claims to having actually achieved anything new with that book, nor do I make any claims to have been the first to try. The only claim I make is that I was looking to *try* something new, and, by my own standards at least, I succeeded. And it was thanks to those artists, some of them obscure, most of them reviled, many of them accused of being talentless frauds, displayed in the contemporary-art rooms at the National Gallery that I had the courage to try.

III

It has been ten years since I first found out I had HIV, got out of treatment, and fell in love, or in thrall, to modern and contemporary art. So much has happened since. I have changed cities, partners, careers. I got a dog, and my two cats have grown old and lazy. I have found some success as a writer — enough at least to know that this is what I want to continue doing with my life. And yet there was a period after writing *June* that I despaired of ever writing anything good again.

Once you start breaking all the rules and flaunting tradition — where do you go from there? Do you go backwards and retreat into tradition? Do you stay stuck where you are, only to repeat yourself endlessly? Ironically, the liberating experience of freeing myself entirely from the traditions of my forefathers paralyzed me for a time more effectively than externally imposed rules of composition ever could. The one thing I did not want to do was write another novel like my first two, *Tyler's Cape* or *Still Life with June*, even if the subject was different, if the shape stayed the same. There are sequels in form and style as well as sequels in material content; as Jeanette Winterson says, sequels are for writers who have run out of ideas. As an antidote to this, I continued to haunt modern-art galleries, hoping that, as sometimes happens, in the poison I would find the cure. I travelled a great deal — London, Paris, Rome, New York, Barcelona, Brussels, Tokyo and Bangkok — but it was in my old standby, the National Gallery of Canada, that the second revelation came. Again it was inspired by the art team General Idea and Felix Partz.

I was roaming the halls one Saturday afternoon with a friend of mine, and we stumbled by chance into a darkened section of the gallery that had a closed door at either end. Taking up one entire wall was a giant, backlit photographic portrait of the dark-haired, dark-eyed Partz, propped up — with a phalanx of pillows behind him in his bed — in his home in Vancouver. His eyes were open and he was staring fixedly at the camera. He did not look well. His face was gaunt and terribly thin, his cheeks sunken — a byproduct of the HIV medications that rob fat from the face and deposit it on other parts of the body. A lighted plaque on the wall indicated that Partz was not only sick when the photo was taken, but that he had been dead several hours. He had arranged with his fellow artists to sit him up and photograph him after his death, while rigor mortis was setting in, and then to install the results in the gallery as an artistic swan song, a political statement on AIDS, and a testament to the determination of the artist.

|9

As I had done ten years before with his work, I stood in the centre of a room and I cried over what I saw: the strength it took Partz to chronicle his own death in art, and the subjects available to the contemporary artist if only he has guts enough to face himself down, no matter how unusual or bizarre or isolating his experience. What Partz had done once again was to speak to those of us brave enough to listen, and perhaps even those few of us with HIV who knew someday we too, like him, would die of AIDS and end up looking like this on our own deathbeds. Not a pretty statement, but a powerful one.

"Jesus Christ," whispered my friend, when he realized what we were looking at.

"Jesus Christ is right," I said.

I went home that day strangely refreshed, and started writing something new that very evening. Now, whenever I am worried I will run out of ideas, I simply think of Felix Partz, and keep working.

THE VARIOUS NAMES OF GOD

I first told my father I was gay in the summer of 1987, when I was nineteen years old. Those seem like dim dark days to me now, ancient history, when I was still living at home in the tiny village of Greenfield, Nova Scotia during the summers and attending liberal-arts classes at university during the spring, winter, and fall. I met my first boyfriend that June, on my very first visit to a gay bar on Halifax's seedy and occasionally dangerous Gottingen Street. I had a few drinks at a friend's apartment, walked down in the general direction of my destination, and then did not have the courage to go in. Instead, I slipped into a seedy diner across the street, where for two hours an overweight black waitress in a blue uniform served me rum-and-cokes without ice in plastic cups. When I ordered my sixth or seventh drink and was getting too loaded to go anywhere, she looked at me and said, "It's okay, honey. No one's gonna bite you. Just *go!*"

"Go where?" I said, feigning ignorance.

She put her hands on her hips, the way the black women in Nova Scotia who have learned the hard way not to take any bullshit off anybody do, and said, "Where do you think? To the goddamned fruit bar, honey. You *know* that's where you want to be."

Thus admonished, I paid my bill, climbed unsteadily off my stool, and did as I was told. My biggest fear (and what the more than half dozen rum-and-cokes were ingested to counteract) was the fear of running into someone I knew. And, as if that God I no longer believed in was enjoying himself immensely at my expense, less than five drunken feet into the door I met my old high-school biology teacher, Mr. M, coming out of the bathroom near the entrance. I nearly fainted. "What in the hell are you doing here?" he said, looking just as shocked as I felt.

Our mutual discomfort didn't last for long. The great truth about running into someone you know upon your first visit to a gay bar is that they are just as scared of running into you. Mr. M took me under his wing, and introduced me to his friends. One of these was John, an elementary school teacher, who became my lover for the next year and taught me all the ins and outs of being gay in Nova Scotia. (This included the very painful lesson that no relationship, however much you want it, can last forever.)

The Friday evening, months later, that I told my father I was gay, I was back in Greenfield, preparing to drive down to Mr. M's cottage outside the town of Bridgewater, thirty kilometres away, where I would spend the weekend on the lake with my gay friends and my lover. Somehow, my father found out about this. Since it was rumoured in our village that Mr. M was gay, and I was going to his cottage for the weekend, he was beginning to suspect that all was not well, or normal, with his nineteen-year-old son. From this distance of time and experience, I can understand how he must have agonized over this, how the worry of it likely kept him awake at night, preyed on his mind, burned his gut like poisonous bile. I hardly thought of these things at all. I was too busy anticipating my weekend in the arms of someone I thought I loved, and being with friends who accepted me for who I was and what I wanted.

* * *

In Greenfield there was an event called the Woodsmen's Competition that took place for two weeks every August. This was a huge annual deal for our little village. For two weekends in a row it drew thousand of spectators from all over the Maritimes, and performers from as far away as Scotland and Louisiana. It was a Scottish-style affair, with log-rolling and pole-climbing and sawing and peavey-pitching competitions. Tanned and brawny mustachioed men in jean coveralls and black-and-red checked shirts (which we always referred to, for some reason, as doe-skins) competed in the most masculine, the most heterosexual, of events. My father worked for the Nova Scotia Power Corporation and climbed power poles for a living. So, each year, he entered the pole-climbing competition, for which he practised for months beforehand, and was always very proud to compete with all these rugged professionals, though he always came in close to dead-last in the final tallies.

That Friday was my father's big night. It was my big night also, for I was to be paid fifty dollars to play my guitar and sing at the festival beer tent, after which my boyfriend would pick me up and we would make a quick escape back to my former teacher's cottage. It was about six o'clock in the evening. My mother was still at work; my father and I were sitting at the kitchen table having a lemonade and taking a breather before our respective performances.

But my father had other things on his mind. He asked me where I was going that night, and when I told him, he said, "You know Mr. M is queer."

"I know."

"Are you queer?"

It's funny how things turn out. I had known I was gay since I was thirteen, perhaps before, and somehow I always knew that one day the truth would have to come out. I had spent my own share of restless, sleepless nights agonizing over different scenarios — the various ways that my parents would find out. In most versions, I sat them down and told them, after preparing for months, perhaps years, what I would say. Never once in all these scenarios did I imagine my father asking me that one, simple question.

I seized the opportunity. "Yes," I said defiantly. "I'm queer. So what?"

For the life of me, I can't remember the aftermath of this, or what my father said. I do know that ten minutes later he and I were standing upstairs in my room shouting at each other. He suggested that I could go to therapy; I insisted, as most of us do, that it was not a disease. Eventually I took my guitar and stormed out of the house and left my father alone. I played at the beer tent as planned. In fact, I played exceptionally well, and tried not to give my father a second thought, though I wasn't always successful. I found out years later that he did not compete in his beloved pole-climbing event that evening. He was too distraught. Instead he stayed home and, as I suspect and sometimes even imagine, cried over the news I had given him. (My father and mother have always been people who cry fairly easily, and have never been afraid of showing their tears.)

14 |

After my gig, I went with my boyfriend back to Mr. M's cottage, and we spent a drunken, sexually intense weekend together. I told my friends the story of my father and they all commiserated; they were older and had been through similar situations themselves. On Sunday I came home, hung over and, as usual in those days after a weekend of gay sex, a little ashamed of myself.

That night at dinner my father and I avoided each other's gaze and hardly spoke, even to say "Pass the salt". For the next two weeks the two of us coexisted uneasily in that house, never mentioning the incident or my recent admission, barely speaking beyond the necessary communication. My mother was as garrulous as ever, and from this I concluded that she didn't know. It would be another eight years before she was to hear directly from my lips that I was gay, and that would be through the medium of television, when I appeared on the TV show *Canada AM* and told two million other people at the same time. But that is another story. Suffice it to say that by the time September came, and I was to go back to Halifax and my second year of university, both my father and I were tremendously relieved.

We had one huge fight just before I left, when, at my mother's insistence, he picked me up late one Sunday night from a bar in another nearby town where I had drunk too much to drive home. We said a lot of things on the half-hour drive back to Greenfield, none of it pleasant. I won't repeat it all here — it's too painful, and most of the things we said were not meant; it would be unfair to both of us to record them.

The crux of it, however, was that I didn't respect him, that I would never be able to respect him.

He said that he didn't respect me, either.

"Therein lies our problem," I said.

"I can't wait till you leave. I hope you never come back."

It was a long while before I could forgive my father for saying that, though at the time a part of me knew that he couldn't have meant it truly.

II

What has always surprised me about stories like these, the sad coming-out tales of gay men and women, is their utter uniformity. Whenever I am called upon to tell my story, whether in private or at a public gathering, I am always greeted by the knowing nods of gay men and women who have been through exactly the same thing themselves. The coming-out movies we watched and the novels we read when younger were, originally, so affecting and gut-wrenching precisely because of how strongly we identified with the events unfolding in the fictional worlds before us. I could have written some of the scenes and dialogue for *The Lost Language of Cranes* or *Parting Glances* or the *World of Normal Boys* or *Get Real* myself, so accurate is the correlation between these stories and the events of my own life.

It occurs to me that the coming-of-age stories of heterosexuals are so enduringly popular because they are so varied; the primary fact of a homosexual's existence is the hiding of our secret sexual selves and the purposeful obfuscation of a key aspect of our personalities, as so many of my gay brothers and sisters have done and continue to do. I realized in my early twenties that while a few of the specific details of my upbringing and adolescence were mine and mine alone, the central narrative of my childhood, hiding my sexuality and at the same time gradually coming to terms with it, had already been told, and told well. Ironically, I could not now write a novel specifically about coming out, because of the homogeneity of the coming-out experience.

These novels and stories are still being written, and many of us still identify with them. But as a writer, I am not capable of spending years telling a story that has already been told, even if that story is heavily seasoned with my own experience. *My* coming-out novel is dead. If I want to tell that story, I need to find another way into it, another focus, beyond the story of the missing or hidden selves. I feel slightly robbed of this experience. But it occurs to me that the prevalence of the coming-out story and the reluctant but progressive mainstream acceptance of the homosexual lifestyle in Western society means there is a new reality emerging for gay men and women, and a new kind of story to tell. This excludes, of course, the backslide into inequality fuelled by the Christian right in the United States.

17

It is my belief that the gay story of the new millennium will not be the struggle for self-acceptance and the public acknowledgement of our right to love who we wish; rather, it will be the struggle to define ourselves within the context of a society that no longer cares who we sleep with and marry. This struggle is the great modern struggle, the search for self-definition, the redefining of the self without the moral codes and religious definitions of the previous centuries, and I believe gay literature will become much more universal than it has been. For most straight men and women, the gay and lesbian coming-out story, no matter how well written, has been little more than an intellectual titillation — a self-righteous testament to their own liberality or a voyeuristic peep into another sexual reality. Even the best of these stories has remained underground sensations, viewed mostly by other gay and lesbian audiences. But gay literature is becoming more mainstream than ever. Three of the five novels nominated for the Amazon.ca/*Books in Canada* First Novel Award in 2002 were by openly gay authors. When you pick up the review section of any major newspaper in Canada, you're likely to find that at least one novel, and likely more, reviewed within its pages has a gay character and/or is written by a gay author. Gay novels such as the Booker Prize winning *The Line of Beauty* have become so universal because the struggle for identity has become so central to the ultra-modern psyche. Along with novels written about the immigrant experience, gay novels have become a metaphor for the isolation and alienation we all feel in the modern world. And thus, the coming-out novel is dead precisely because it was a marginalized literature, meant for a marginalized audience. We have, suddenly, moved from the margins to the centre, and the alienated voice of the gay man and woman echoes the alienated voice for us all.

* * *

This is not to say that there are not pockets of resistance. I write this on the eve of gay marriage being legalized in Canada. Alberta doesn't want it. Ralph Klein, the Alberta premier and a one-man bastion of neo-conservatism, has said that gays can just leave his province if they want to get married. Stephen Harper and the new Conservative-Alliance Party, showing their Social Credit/Reform/ Christian right-wing roots, have proposed legislation to parliament trying to restrict the definition of marriage to a man and a woman to "defend the sanctity of the institution." In the past, whenever repressive legislation was enacted, or defended, it was almost always in the cause of "the defence" of something. For a long while my father was in one of these pockets. I did not, like so many people I know, choose not to speak to my family after my father and I were on the outs. I still went home for visits. I lived with them for a year or so again, and I called a lot and visited every Christmas, even after I moved away to Ottawa. For eight years after the night my father and I said those awful things to each other, our relationship was strained and distant. We simply did not discuss my being gay. I sanitized that part of my life, and so my parents knew only one part of me, the safe acceptable part — the least interesting part of any person.

| 19

But in 1995, I made another trip home to come out all over again. I had been diagnosed HIV-positive that May, and, although I had been warned against it by countless friends and professional advisors, I wanted to go home and tell my parents about my condition. Although I didn't realize it then, I know now that I wanted to see how they would react. I wanted confirmation that they cared about me, that I mattered to them, now that I was facing this new threat.

I told my father first. I waited until my mother went to bed the second night I was home, and then blurted it out. He sobbed. He said he didn't want me to die. He pounded his fists against the wall and cried out the various names of God. The next morning I told my sister. (I left my father to tell my mother, for I didn't think I could face another outpouring of emotion.) The day after, I left for Ottawa again.

After that, my father and I started speaking to each other more, and, in 1997, he came up for a visit and stayed with me at my apartment. This happened to coincide with the gay pride march in the city. The day before, entirely on the spur of the moment, I asked my father if he wanted to go. He was hesitant at first. He thought people would throw rocks at us, and boo and hiss and make fun of us. Eventually he agreed, and was surprised, I think, when the next morning on the streets of Ottawa there was none of what he'd feared and imagined. The world had moved on while he was cloistered away in his little village; and once he realized he was not going to be denigrated for having a gay son, he was free to enjoy himself.

20 |

To this day my father tells me what a good time he had. He marched proudly with me and my friends (one of whom, my friend Steve, was attired in a dress and high heels, still sporting his radical fairy's beard.) He even handed out condoms and safe-sex pamphlets as a favour to one of the AIDS organizations marching behind us. He targeted people on the sidelines who, as he put it, "look a little afraid, like I used to be." Afterwards we went to a gay bar and watched a drag show. The day after, I drove my father to the airport where we hugged and he got on a plane for Nova Scotia. I'll never forget what he whispered in my ear just before he pulled away and disappeared through the passenger security gates.

"It's alright that you're gay," he said. He wasn't giving *me* permission. He was giving it to himself.

III

As I write this my father turns sixty. I have become a novelist, and, though I don't like to be called a gay novelist, I make no secret about my sexuality. My books have gay characters. I talk about being gay on TV and radio, in newspaper articles and on the Internet. Recently, I went to my old high school to give a copy of my new novel to one of the more encouraging English teachers I had there. In the hallway of the school I ran into my old friend, Mr. M, who was now in his fifties and close to retiring but still teaching at that very same school. The two of us went out for a quick lunch and we talked about the weekend I told my father I was gay. (The old boyfriend John is long since gone and forgotten).

"Your father has completely turned around," M told me. "I see him now, and he's so proud of you and the books you're writing. I don't think you could find a prouder man on this whole planet."

"I know. He even tells waiters and waitresses at restaurants we go to that I'm a published writer."

M and I laughed and ate our pizza. Later we drove back to the school and I spent a pleasant afternoon in the teacher's lounge with old familiar faces.

At four o'clock I drove back to my parents' house where my father, now retired from the power corporation and too old to climb poles anymore, sat at the kitchen table watching my mother prepare a meal. I sat down with him. We talked about my visit to the school, and my book, and Mr. M. "The old troublemaker," my father called him, and we laughed.

We ate dinner, and afterward everyone else disappeared outside, or into the living room to watch television. My father and I sat across from each other at our old stomping grounds, the kitchen table. There was still that distance between us, perhaps the result of damage done that can never be repaired. Or it simply may be the distance that exists between all fathers and sons, divided as we are by geography and history, generations and language, and time. And yet, despite all this, the silence in the kitchen managed to be comfortable, as the lemon-tinged light of the afternoon melted into the solemn blue shadows of yet another Nova Scotia evening.

MY FATHER'S
DREAMS

My father started work on a novel when I was twelve years old. He would come home from work as a lineman for the Nova Scotia Power Corporation. He would have dinner, and then, after the dishes were cleaned and put away, and the family had retired to the living room to watch TV, he would pull out the skeletal, black cast-iron Underwood typewriter. An aunt had given him this antique years ago; it weighed more than I did at the time. He would place it on the kitchen table, sit down, roll a clean, white sheet of paper into its platen and start typing. For months he did this, and we would have to turn up the TV, for the old Underwood was noisy and my father had never learned how to type. He used two fingers and pounded the keys so hard a blind person, by tracing his fingers over the underside of the paper, would likely have been able to fathom what he wrote there.

My father would never tell us anything about the novel, not even its title.

"Can we read it?" my brother, sister and I would always ask him.

"Not until it's published and I've made a million dollars."

When you're twelve, even a somewhat insecure, cynical twelve-year-old, statements like these do not seem odd. The possibility that my father could get his novel published and make a million dollars from it did not seem at all outlandish to me then. I simply shrugged my shoulders and went back to my TV show, certain that one day I would get to read it. Meanwhile, the stack of papers beside my father's elbow began to grow. Each day, he told us, he planned while he was at work what he was going to write about, and each night he stayed at it, sometimes until ten or eleven o'clock, long past our bedtime. My mother showed little interest in my father's project. A couple of times she called him a "silly fool" when he went on about money or fame (my mother has always been the hard-headed realist in our family) but most nights she didn't say anything when he pulled out the Underwood. We were uncertain if my mother had read the book — many things went on behind the closed door of their bedroom at night that we knew nothing about — but she never mentioned it. And when my father started dragging out the typewriter less and less often at night, claiming exhaustion or simply a lack of inspiration that evening, she never mentioned that either. I had been writing for a number of years, and I knew that my father was succumbing to that malady known to all writers, young or old — the waning of enthusiasm for the story you're telling. Sometimes the illness is temporary, because your mind, or whatever organ is responsible for the telling of stories, just needs a break and time to recharge its batteries before getting back to the fictional world. But at other times, in my father's case, the illness is fatal; the manuscript dies.

* * *

My father went through a period around this time when he was looking for a way to escape the reality of his own circumstances. It was not the typical mid-life crisis; life for our family was more complicated than it was for other people, or at least it seemed that way from the inside. My father had come from an adopted family; he had gone into the navy at a young age and developed a drinking problem. He gave up drinking one afternoon when he stole the last thirty dollars from my mother's purse — money she had been saving for groceries. When he came home that evening, drunk on the money he had stolen, she was waiting for him at the door with my infant brother in her arms, my sister and I in our jackets and shoes, our bags packed.

"I'm leaving you," she told him.

My father begged her not to go. He even went so far as to get down on his knees. Surprisingly my mother, who like her own mother was never one for second chances, agreed to stay.

"But it's the booze or us," she said. "You give up one, or you lose the other."

Miraculously, my father listened and started going to AA. He was unfamiliar with the program, so he didn't think anything was out of the ordinary that the group was "led" by one man who, week after week, held forth about his own life and times and philosophy on living sober, and never once gave anyone else a chance to speak. My father drifted away from the group and somehow still managed to stay sober.

About a year after this, our house burned to the ground while my father was away on a trip with his work. We didn't have any insurance, so we moved into a one-room apartment in another part of town. Then we moved into a bigger apartment on Court

Street, and a year later, when I was eight, my parents bought the 130-year-old farmhouse in the village of Greenfield. By then, my father had three kids, a wife, a mortgage, a dead-end job that paid just enough to make it difficult to leave, and a whole head full of might-have-beens.

Social standing has always been important to my father. Growing up, we were most likely to get into trouble when we did something that might embarrass us. At dinner, when we had a kind of family meeting around our kitchen table, my mother would recount the day's exploits, including our behavior (which was rarely, if ever, good), and he would say to us, "What do the goddamned neighbours think?"

We didn't care, nor did they. Our neighbour to the north was J.J. — a mean old man who wouldn't let us pick blueberries in his field and once shot our dog in the hind leg and seriously wounded him. J.J. had been in the Second World War, and had returned a little "fucked up in the head" — Nova Scotia speak for shell-shocked. Across the ball diamond, on the other side of us, were the Fs, a family of raucous, violent-tempered men and women who would shout and scream at each other for hours each evening and on drunken Saturday nights fire off guns into the air for the joy of it. Although we didn't say anything to my father, the neighbours likely never even looked twice at us, and if they did, it was probably through the sights of a gun.

But my father laboured under the recovering alcoholic's misconception that everyone was looking at us, taking notes, so we had to act accordingly. He was ashamed of his job. He'd always wanted to be a desk worker, to wear a suit to work. A suit demanded respect. A friend of mine told me once that his father thought the same thing, and had asked his son, who was a roofer, why he didn't get some education and wear a suit and make something of himself. "Dad," my friend said. "Some of the biggest crooks in the world wear a three-piece suit to work every day."

Touché, but the point was lost on my friend's dad. As it would have been lost on my father, had I made it. He wore denim coveralls to work. When he came home he smelled of the distilled essence of hard labour — sweat and grease and cigarette smoke. He cursed those at work who were keeping him down, and was always planning ways to "get the hell out of there."

The failed novel was one way.

Selling pots and pans was another.

Somewhere along the line my father met up with a man who owned a company that sold stainless-steel pots and pans at $800 a set. The sales pitch was rather ingenious. First, the salesman would come into a house and cook the family's dinner in the pots. The meal was always the same — red cabbage, steak, oven-baked potatoes, and asparagus — and over dinner the salesman would give his pitch. The crux of the pitch was based on some phony studies that aluminum pots, which most people still used in those days, were responsible for Alzheimer's disease.

It was a good pitch, and the company was doing well, or so said Dale, the owner, who had taken to driving down from Halifax in his new Camaro and spending hours talking to my father about "the biz." Soon my father began selling for him on weekends. The fridge was always stuffed with these untouchables — the cabbage, steak and specially prepared potatoes. After work on Friday, he would change out of his coveralls, shower and dress in a suit, and off he would go, a box of food under his arm. He actually sold a few sets (my father is a very charming man when he wants to be, and likely *would* have made a good salesman), and it wasn't long before he was talking about leaving his job at the Nova Scotia Power Corporation and working full-time for Dale, the pot-seller. This was one of the bigger crises I remember having in our house.

My mother was practical, and she had pretty much all that she'd ever wanted — a home of her own, a car, three reasonably healthy children, and enough money to live on and to put a little aside. She had a vision that included sending us to university if we wanted to go, fixing up the house, retiring, and travelling one day to New York to see the Yankees in Yankee Stadium (she was a big baseball fan, even then, before the Blue Jays won the World Series twice). Her vision did not include fame and fortune; it certainly did not include Dale, his Camaro, his pots and pans, and his get-rich-quick schemes. For weeks she fought with my father over his new plan. He argued that he was unhappy, that he wanted to "make something of himself."

She told him that they had commitments — a mortgage and three children. Could he see his way to making something of that?

"I'm stuck in this dead-end fucking job that I hate," was my father's most common rejoinder. "I have an opportunity to turn things around, and you're worried about the mortgage?"

"What about the kids? What about college for Darren? What about clothes and food and vacation and fixing up the house and all the things we've been working towards?"

"We'll be rich," my father said weakly. "I'll be my own boss, don't you see?"

For weeks these words echoed throughout the house every night, sometimes in low, insistent tones, at other times at the top of my mother's or father's lungs. It got so bad that I, along with my sister and brother, actually started listening to it. At the tender ages of twelve, eleven and eight, we began to worry about our family's financial security.

"Don't quit your job, Dad," I remember saying once to my father. "We don't want to be poor."

How difficult that must have been — the entire family against him! And then my mother did something she had not done before. She brought in an outsider. She asked my Aunt Gert, recently widowed and the most well-off of my many relatives, to talk to my father. My Aunt Gert agreed, and came up with a compromise. My father would retire at the age of fifty (he was then forty-two), and when he did, my aunt would invest in any business he wanted to run.

This clinched it. My father gave in, and the next time Dale came down, my father told him he couldn't sell for him full-time. Dale was disappointed, and told my father so. Only a few months later, Dale stopped coming around and my father stopped selling pots and pans for him. We heard that Dale went bankrupt and got into some kind of legal trouble over the company, though my mother, bless her heart, refrained from telling my father, "I told you so."

My father went back to work, though he did not give up his schemes entirely. He ended up investing in and thinking up ideas for a lot of companies over the years. The one I remember most vividly, after the pot-selling venture, was his investment in a gold mine run by this crazy man from Halifax named Brian. Brian was reviving the abandoned mines at Molega a few miles from our house. He had gold fever worse than any man that my father (or anybody else from Greenfield) had ever met, but his ambitions died with him when he was asphyxiated, having gone down into a mineshaft without proper ventilation.

Needless to say, none of these plans came to anything, and my father retired, almost as projected, from the Power Corporation at age fifty-two, though by then my aunt had little or no money left and was in no position to fund any business venture of his. He started his own company anyway, and has had some moderate success as a contractor for the same corporation that used to employ him. He doesn't make much more money than he did when he worked for them directly, but he is his own boss, and he sometimes wears a suit to work, which is really all he ever wanted.

* * *

When I was sixteen years old, I found the stack of papers my father had been working on when he tried to write his novel. There was a closet off my parents' bedroom where they put most everything they didn't want us to find — Christmas presents, important papers, valuable items like my father's antique camera, the Underwood, a red-lacquered mahogany bone-key accordion that my father was convinced would be worth a fortune someday. Somewhere in that closet was also a secret compartment that my younger brother had told my sister and me was there — a sort of built-in wooden safe where most of the *really* secret items were kept. For years we searched for this compartment — in the walls, in the floors, in the ceiling of the closet. It became a grail of sorts, and we all used to take time out of our day when my parents were away to poke around in the closet looking for Christmas presents and hunting for "the safe." Even my youngest brother would do this, though years later he told us he had made the story up, but somehow, in the telling of it, he had convinced himself as well.

When I was twelve, I was certain the safe was where my father kept the novel he had been working on for those few months; by the time I came upon the book four years later I had almost forgotten about it. We never did find his hiding place and probably | 31 would not have found the book if he hadn't left it out on the shelf above where my mother kept her shoes. Maybe he had pulled it out to read it again. Or perhaps he was considering reviving it, the way that crazy Brian had tried to revive the Molega gold mines. Whatever the reason, there it was, in plain sight when I opened the closet door, and I recognized it instantly as my father's long-lost book.

My mother had taken a job by then, at a home for the aged in the next little village, and so she and my father were not home when we returned from school. I took the manuscript into the living room, lay down on the sofa, and started reading.

It was titled *Mind Games*, and almost from the first I knew that behind the thin layer of fiction was the story of my father's life.

It was not particularly well-written. I knew that my father would never make a million dollars off this, even if he did manage to get it published, which I doubted. (All writers have an uncanny knack for knowing when the writing of others sucks, though we frequently can't bring this faculty to bear on our own work). But I was fascinated anyway: for here, in my father's own words, was the story of his life, without the usual gloss, edits, or omissions.

I read about his childhood, and how he felt, and all the things he did.

I read about his children, and what he thought of us (it wasn't always flattering or entirely paternal either).

I read about his job, and who was doing what to whom (including sexually, which was most interesting).

I was shocked when the lead character admitted to hiring prostitutes when he was away on his business trips from his wife and kids, and it was at this point that I became uncomfortable and put the manuscript back. I knew what my father wrote was true, and that he had done these things. I know now, of course, that it is the writer's role to learn such uncomfortable secrets about his family and the world — to carry these inside him until they have to come out in the form of fiction (or essays such as these). At the time, I felt horrified that I knew such an intimate, shocking thing about my father, and yet, I also felt oddly comforted, perhaps because, through the dirt, I was finally able to see my father as just human.

My mother did not feel the same way when she discovered the manuscript later that afternoon when she returned from work. She had gone into the closet and had seen it lying exactly where I had found it, on the shelf above her shoes. She too couldn't resist; she read the book, what there was of it, and when my father came home an hour later she was waiting for him. My mother wasn't fooled by the characters' names either; if my father's desire to sell pots and pans was the worst sustained crisis of our household during my childhood, this was the worst single fight.

My brother, sister and I cowered upstairs while my parents screamed at each other and said the most horrible things. Only I knew exactly what they were screaming about, for I knew my mother was confronting him in veiled terms (so we children wouldn't catch on) about the prostitutes. This time my mother made good on her threat made so many years earlier; she packed her bags and left. My sister ran downstairs sobbing and begged her not to go, but it did no good. She went away for the first time in the history of our family, and did not return for three days. When she did come back, persuaded by the same aunt who had talked my father years before into not leaving his job, she did not speak to my father for a month, and was morose and difficult with us. |33 Finally, one night at the dinner table when my mother was silently eating and still refusing to look at any of us, my father got up, went into his bedroom, and returned a few minutes later with the manuscript in hand. He opened the front door, and in plain view of us all, laid the stack of papers on the front step, pulled a lighter out of his pocket, and set the manuscript afire.

We all watched it burn, my father standing above it, my mother and her children still sitting at the kitchen table. "Clean up the ashes," my mother told him after the fire had burnt itself out. He swept them up into the dustpan and dumped them in the fireplace in the yard. Then he came back in and sat down wordlessly at the table. My mother, who had been crying, wiped her eyes with her napkin and told us all to finish our supper.

Which we did, in utter silence.

It is only now that I recognize this as the exact moment when my father's dreams of being a writer died, and my own began in earnest.

STRANGE
GHOSTS

My father was born on March 12, 1944 at Saint Joseph's Hospital in Toronto. His mother was sixteen years old when she had him, and whether she was forced, convinced, or decided on her own to give him up on that day makes little difference now. If she is still alive, she would be seventy-six, and my father has given up looking for her.

The name given my father when he was born was Beverly Gordon, the first of which has caused him some minor embarrassment his entire life. The family who raised him in the small Ontario town of Palgrave, which is just north of Toronto, called him by his middle name, Gordon; later, in high school, he was given the nickname "Charcoal Charlie," because of his skin colour, and when he got into the navy the nickname stuck. He introduced himself to my mother as Charlie and this is how I know him.

The years spent with his foster family in small-town Ontario my father has kept deliberately sketchy. I know he had two older foster brothers. There are photographs of my father at twelve, dressed in hand-me-down shoes, faded work pants, and a black-and-white-checked shirt, standing on the side of a country road, shielding his eyes from the sun and smiling shyly at the camera. From the hints my father has dropped, it is clear that his older brothers let no chance pass by for the careful instruction of their foster brother. Based on a meeting I had with one of them, and the way my father has spoken of them over the years, I can gather that beneath this instruction and seeming goodwill was layered much resentment and even some contempt, and that my father was a second-class citizen in the country of his own family.

The one thing the Gibsons did give my father was a lifelong love of the game of hockey. Both Gibson boys were on one team or another, as was my father. When I was growing up, he spent most of his Saturday nights in the hockey arena in Liverpool, Nova Scotia, and he played on a team well into his fifties. For a few short years, my father was the oldest member of his local Old-Timers hockey league. (This tradition continues in our family — my nephew Nathan, my sister's oldest boy, is as crazy about hockey as my father was and plays defence on his team in the same arena his grandfather used to play in.)

I know he loved his foster mother, and that he was heartbroken when she died. He was twelve, the age at which that single surviving photograph of him was taken.

I also know that the kids in school made fun of him and called him names because he was so dark-skinned, and that for many years he had no idea from what race or people he was descended. His foster family told him he was Italian, and for thirty years he would go around telling people this, even though the Italians he met didn't think he looked like them at all. At a young age, my father started skipping school and hanging out at the local snooker hall, smoking cigarettes, and learning to sink red and white and yellow balls into green-felt pockets. At sixteen, he quit school and took a part-time job repairing Wurlitzer jukeboxes. He started to drink.

I know that, disgusted with my father's behaviour, and he with theirs, the Gibsons called the Children's Aid Society into their house when my father turned eighteen. When the Society representative asked what the family wanted to do with him, my foster grandfather said, "We want him out."

| 37

It was decided then and there that my father would be sent off to the navy, which in those days took any man who could walk a straight line sober and could count to twenty without taking his shoes off. My father had no prospects — no money, no education, no family other than his foster one, who had never taken that extra step and adopted him — and so he had no choice. He was sent down to his local recruiting office and forced to join up. In August 1962, my father was driven to the Toronto airport by his father and the Gibson boys and put on a plane for boot camp in Cornwallis, Halifax. By some small twist of irony, the only other boy leaving for boot camp that day was a young Italian man, whose entire extended family had gathered at the airport to see him off. My father remembers the contrast to this day. There stood the Gibsons in a tight, silent, anxious knot while their foster son stood nervously apart, waiting for his call to board. Beside him stood the Italian boy, whose family cried and hugged and kissed and shouted and exclaimed over him. Someone from the Italian family noticed my father, and to his surprise, and to the surprise, I'm sure, of the Gibsons, pulled him into the fray and started hugging and kissing and crying and exclaiming over him as well, even though they didn't know him from Adam. Or Michelangelo.

I believe, though my father has never said so, that he remembers this incident so well because it was the first time anyone in his life had ever demonstrated any kind of love toward him. My father got on the plane, and it would be a lifetime before he came back to Ontario again.

II

In 1996, when I was in a Salvation Army Treatment Centre in Ottawa, my father flew up from Halifax. He was still playing hockey then, and his team was involved in a tournament in Nepean. It was winter. Ottawa, as usual, was freezing. On the first night he arrived, we went for dinner at a restaurant on Elgin Street. My parents had had a few months to adjust to the fact that I was now a self-proclaimed addict in recovery. In between 12-Step meetings and group therapy, I was attending literature courses at Carleton University and working on my first novel. My father was just glad I had a few dollars in the bank and wasn't "wasting my life" anymore.

After dinner, over coffee, he told me that he had been in touch with the Children's Aid Society of Ontario about his birth family, and had discovered he was not Italian as he had been told. He was Aboriginal. I often credit my obsession with the subject of hidden identity in my writing to my father and his story. All through my childhood growing up in the small WASP-ish community of Greenfield, it was an issue, as people endlessly wondered about my family's skin colour. My sister and father are dark; my brother and I, lighter. The townspeople wondered, as the racist expression goes, what was "in the woodpile." We told everyone what my father had been told, that we were Italian, and I don't suppose the Gibsons ever realized that their "white" lie would become a generational myth, its effects reverberating down through fifty years and two generations, affecting dozens of lives. We so heavily invested in the Italian theory that spaghetti night was a regular occurrence at our house, and my father would often shout out "Mama Mia!" in the middle of the meal and make us all laugh.

And then, suddenly, we weren't Italian anymore. We were Aboriginal, a somewhat murkier proposition, even in 1996.

In some ways, it made sense.

Years before, my father had developed a minor obsession with Aboriginal culture. He ordered a whole series of Time-Life books from television about Aboriginal peoples, and he used to sit and pore over the pictures of these books for hours in his living room chair, perhaps never dreaming that he was looking at photos of his distant ancestors.

At the time I was in treatment, one of my friends, the Ojibwa novelist Richard Wagamese, was teaching me about Aboriginal culture, and I had begun to smudge myself with burning sweet grass, cedar, and sage in my room in the centre at night (though I kept quiet about it, as it was considered a pagan ritual, and so was technically not allowed inside the Christian-run complex). Although it took me a long while to identify publicly as Aboriginal (something I still find hard to do), I began to attend Aboriginal healing circles and ceremonies after my father shared his news, and began volunteering and working for Aboriginal organizations. I already had many Aboriginal friends, who were now eager to bring me back into the fold and teach me about the culture that had been taken away from me, so the psychological transition from European to Aboriginal North American, at least on a private level, was fairly easy for me. My father was deeply Christian by the time he found out who he was, and was unwilling to give that up. Many Aboriginal people in Nova Scotia are also Christian, thanks to four hundred years of conversion efforts on the part of Christian missionaries, and so this is not a great problem where my father lives. He has managed to partially accept his Aboriginal heritage, and mix it with his fervent Christian beliefs, as so many others have done before him.

My brother, as far as I know, has never mentioned an ancestry, and my sister, on the few occasions we have discussed it, has been downright hostile to the idea. At one point, she insisted that we simply don't know what we are. I didn't bother to argue with her. Identity is such a personal thing, and I think my sister still struggles with the fact that kids used to call her "squaw" and "Injun" when she was little because with her brown skin and long braided dark hair she looked so much like a little Aboriginal girl.

My mother, as usual in our family, put it best. "Here we were," she said, "thinking we were Italians all these years, and eating all that goddamned spaghetti, and it turns out we were big ol' Indians. What in the world do Indians eat?"

Bannock.

I found it touching at the time, and still do, that my mother is so attached to my father that she includes herself in this identity shift, even thought her blood is pure Scotch-Irish by birth. My mother's family, who at first did not like my father but who, over the years, have gained a grudging respect for him, were not that surprised.

"I always knew he was *something!*" said my grandmother. "Makes sense that he's one of *that bunch.*"

"That bunch" was my grandmother's way of referring, in general, to anyone who was Indian and, specifically, to the Mi'kmaw family that had lived across the street from my grandmother's house for most of my mother's childhood. My grandmother always referred to them as "that bunch of Indians," and they always referred to my mother's family, thanks to my grandfather's genes and original province, as "that bunch of bald-headed Newfoundlanders."

When my grandmother found out about my father, she dropped "of Indians" from her phrase and simply referred to anyone who was Aboriginal as "that bunch."

Even among the very aged, political correctness can find a toehold.

III

The Italian boy my father went to naval camp with lasted only three weeks before he quit and headed back to Ontario to be with his family. My father has often wondered aloud what became of him. My father stayed in the navy. As has often been the case for so many directionless, troubled young men, the regimented life suited him. He was told when to eat, when to drink, when to talk, when to stay quiet, when to work, when to march, and when to sleep. In his time off, he learned to drink like a navy man, which meant drinking a lot.

After boot camp he was sent to sonar school in Dartmouth, and after graduating there, he was berthed on a naval destroyer escort as a sonar operator. He sailed around the world. He went on manoeuvres in Gibraltar, and docked in the Azores and Morocco.

42 | My father tells a funny story about getting drunk with another cadet in Tangiers, donning fezzes and trying to sneak back on board past the guards after missing midnight curfew. They ended up clinging to the rails on the side of the ship, with spotlights and a hundred rifles trained on them, after a guard spotted them and, thinking they were Moroccan spies, called out reinforcements. They spent a week in the brig for their trouble.

My father went to practically every major port in the world, saw most major coastal cities, and, according to his own admission, remembers only the inside of bars, brothels, and the onboard stockade.

In Marseilles, broke and still drunk, he and another friend waded around in a town fountain in the middle of the night filling their pockets with rusted francs. When they dumped them, in still dripping mounds, on the counter in front of the nearest bartender, they found out that France had just switched to the new franc and the old franc was worthless. Out of sympathy, the bartender gave them each a free glass of wine.

In Rio de Janeiro, someone on board came up with the bright idea of paying the prostitutes with Canadian Tire money, and for days the sailors fucked their brains out for free, until word got back to the onboard command. All Canadian Tire money was confiscated and warnings were issued to all the brothels in the city. In every city, there was some shenanigan, some story to tell, but my father has absolutely no memory of the place, the people, the language, the landscape, or the culture. Years later, when I visited many of these places myself, I would often think of my father, blind drunk but strikingly handsome in his naval uniform, strolling the streets arm-in-arm with the other young cadets, all of them bawling out naval ditties at the top of their lungs. My father might have spent many years, or the rest of his life, serving in the navy if he had not met my mother in Halifax, at a dance held in the basement of the Vimy Branch of the Royal Canadian Legion on Cogswell Street. He was on shore leave from his ship, and wearing his midshipman's uniform. My mother, my father admitted to me in one of his franker moments, was wearing a black cocktail dress that gave him a hard-on just looking at her. My father was playing snooker with some of his navy buddies, and after a few more shots of liquid courage he marched up to my mother, who was standing amidst her friends near the bar, and asked her to dance.

"Not fucking likely," she answered.

My mother was not raised, exactly, to be a lady. She swore like a sailor, and for years when I was growing up it was *fuck this* and *fuck that* and *goddamn son-of-a-bitching* something else. Defeated, my father slunk back to the snooker table and his friends, who laughed at him for his failed efforts. But he did not give up. Every hour or so he would go over to my mother's table and — increasingly more aggressive the more he drank — ask her to dance. Finally, at the end of the night, my mother agreed.

"Just to get him out of my hair," she has said.

They danced a fast song, then a waltz, and somewhere in those few minutes my mother gave in and they became a couple. My father spent one more year in the navy. My mother kept her job at a local hospital. They had me, and I was promptly shipped for six months to my grandmother's until my father could get discharged and they could move back to Liverpool to reclaim me (they would have to fight with my grandmother to give me up).

44 | For the first five years of my life my father drank. My earliest memories of him are of riding high on his shoulders up the dirt road from our house to the bootleggers, or being set down in an overstuffed chair when I was four, and having a bottle of beer placed before me because my drunken father decided it was time for me "to be a man." Another memory is of my mother dumping a pot of boiling potatoes over his head and nearly scalding him in the kitchen one Saturday afternoon when he came home drunk from the tavern and sat down at the table and started being difficult with her visiting sisters. He quit drinking when I was five, only to watch the seeds of his alcoholism take hold and sprout in his two sons. My sister suffers from an eating disorder, and so has not escaped this tendency toward disorder that afflicts our family.

For all the years he was sober when we were growing up, he hardly ever mentioned his family, or the navy. Once in a while he would talk about finding his birth mother, but he never made any move to do so. We sometimes wondered from whom we had descended on my father's side, but my mother's family, with her thirteen brothers and sisters and their wives and husbands and their children and their children's children, were all the family we ever needed. But my father, although my mother's family grew to love him, always struck me as a figure set apart and isolated from the rest of us. During the first fifteen years of his sobriety, he was often restless for change, difficult, regretful of the past. He longed for acceptance in our little community of Greenfield, and my mother often complained that he worked harder for a neighbour — so that he would look good in their eyes — than he ever did at home.

I will admit that he tried hard. He took self-improvement courses, and read Dale Carnegie. He became a fervent Christian. He joined the fire department, became a Scout leader, and coached baseball. He briefly considered quitting his job and becoming a salesman. He read history books, tried to write a novel, and built a doghouse for our rambunctious Siberian husky, Skipper. (Skipper destroyed it in a matter of minutes, since my father had built it out of flimsy panelling instead of a more enduring material). He hunted deer and rabbit and played hockey. He tried to be a good father. But there was, and perhaps still is, a core of ineffable sadness in my father. It is the sadness that results from not knowing who he is or where he comes from (a Samuel Beckett-type dilemma if there ever was one).

Then, in 1982, his foster father died, and for the first time since he had left it twenty years before, he flew home to Palgrave, Ontario to attend the funeral. He flew back to Nova Scotia three days earlier than planned, in complete disgust, as his father's sons and their wives were already squabbling over who was going to get what was left of the meagre estate. That was the last time for many years that he had anything to do with his foster family. Each year after that he got a Christmas card with a photocopied, typed newsletter inserted in it from Lenore, his brother Jack's wife, telling him the news of the family. My father still reads these aloud to us each year, and we all suspect that Lenore's policy on what to include is very much like that of Communist China: print the good, ignore the bad.

Two years ago, after he found out he was Aboriginal, my father was put in touch with a half-sister who lives in BC, and she calls my father occasionally to chat. I talked to her on the phone two Christmases ago for the first time. It was odd, talking to this blood relative five thousand miles away, whom I'd never met. I suspect, though he has never said this, that my father feels the same way.

To this day, my father has not found any more of his family. Once, when I was living in Ottawa, I had a phone call from a man looking for Gordon Greer. "Sorry, wrong number," I said, and it was only a second after I hung up that it occurred to me that Gordon is the name everyone knew my father by when he was young. I tried calling the operator back to get the number, but it was blocked and there was no way of retrieving it. I still feel I may have missed by inches uncovering some great mystery that day: that the person I hung up on might have had some clue as to who my father really is.

* * *

In early 2003, my father came by some information, garnered from the hospital in Toronto he was born in, that his mother had listed her address at the time of his birth as 319 Brunswick Avenue in Toronto. He called me up at my apartment and asked me to check it out. I said I would, but for the longest while I kept putting it off. I had just moved to Toronto, was busy promoting my new book and meeting new people, and couldn't be bothered hunting around the city for my father's "strange ghosts," as I'd once described his blood family in a poem I wrote about him. A few months later, it occurred to me that, although he didn't say it, it wasn't just an old house or apartment my father wanted me to look at and describe to him. He was hoping that the woman who had given birth to him all those years ago still lived there.

So up I went to the address my father had given me, in the community known as the Annex, north of Bloor Street. I walked up from my publisher's offices on Spadina, and the closer I got the more excitement I felt. What were the odds that my seventy-six-year-old grandmother lived there still? Slim to none, but I'm not a novelist for nothing. I do believe in hope beyond hope, and coincidences that change our lives. I even imagined myself knocking on the door of an old brownstone and some ancient dark-eyed, dark-skinned woman opening the door and peering out at me with rheumy, near-sighted eyes.

"Do you know Mrs. Greer?" I would ask.

"This is she," the old woman would answer in a weak but puzzled voice, and it would begin, this new chapter to our lives, with the strange ghosts finally made manifest.

When I got to Brunswick Avenue, I quickly realized this wasn't going to happen. The houses on that side of the street went up to 315, there was a small park, and beyond it the addresses started again at 323. There was no 319. I considered for a moment that my father had simply got the address wrong, but I knew he hadn't. I had checked it with him three times, and he, in turn, had checked and rechecked the scrap of paper it was written on.

A man in his mid-fifties, sporting a white beard and wearing faded jeans and a tie-dye T-shirt (a hold-over, I am guessing, from the sixties and my father's golden era of snooker and liquor and

Wurlitzer jukeboxes), was standing on the opposite sidewalk with his hands on his hips, surveying with disapproval an overgrown lawn on his side of the street. I went over and asked him if he knew when the park was built.

"In the seventies," he said.

"And were there houses here once?"

"Yes," he replied, "But they were torn down when they put in the Bloor Subway line, in '63. You'll find most of the houses along here" — he pointed to where the park sat — "were torn down, and parks, or new houses, erected in their place."

It turns out I had run across, in another of those strange coincidences, the former president of the Brunswick Street Residents Association. He knew a lot about the area. I told him I was looking for 319, which my grandmother had been living in when she had given my father up for adoption fifty-nine years ago. The man, who told me his name was Eric, agreed that the park was likely built over that former address, and, indeed, that house would have been torn down to make way for the subway line. An amateur historian warming to his subject, he went on to say that the park was now dedicated to James Tyrell, a nineteenth-century explorer and industrialist. I didn't tell him my initial thought upon hearing this: the holy ghost of the modern age had once more visited us in the fact that such a man should have a park dedicated to him where the former home of a probably long-since-dead Aboriginal woman had once stood. Eric went on to tell me that another Toronto writer, Katherine Govier, used to live on Brunswick Avenue, and that she had written a collection of short stories, the title story of which was about Brunswick Avenue.

"She has a Brunswick Avenue address in that story," said Eric.

"It was written in the eighties, but set in the fifties, so maybe it's the same address you're looking for."

I thanked him and left. After reading the small plaque in the park about James Tyrell, I went to the nearest branch of the public library and asked to see the book of short stories by Katherine Govier. It was in reference, so I couldn't take it out. I found a comfortable chair and sat down with the book; as I did, it occurred to me that my father would likely never find his family. That core of existential loneliness and isolation he felt would probably always remain with him, just as my memories of those first five years when he was always drunk and he and my mother were always fighting are a part of me. On the heels of this thought came the thought that my father had, against all odds, given his children the roots he was never able to claim for himself. Despite all our problems, we know who we are, we know where we come from, and for the most part we know where we are going. "Everyone, at some point in their lives," wrote Katherine Govier, "ends up on Brunswick Avenue."

BASEBALL
AND BAGHDAD

My parents took a plane from Halifax to spend two weeks with me in my apartment, and had done so practically every summer since I first moved to Ottawa in 1994. One of the first things we always did on these visits was to drive to Toronto and see the Blue Jays play at the Sky Dome. My mother had been a committed Blue Jays fan since the eighties, and she never missed an opportunity to see the team in person. She kept an obsessive, near-encyclopaedic track of the players: who had moved up from which farm team, who had been traded from where, who was playing well, and who was not. At the games, she kept meticulous records on the blank scoresheet provided with the program, marking the performance of each player from both teams with a sure-fire knowledge of the shorthand of baseball — K for strikeout, HR for home run, E for error, and BB for base on balls. In the mid-eighties, her favourite player was the wiry, bespectacled pitcher Tom Henke, who was added to the roster in the final innings, to throw his ninety-seven-mile-an-hour fastball by the opposing team's batters and save the game.

"He looks like a geek, doesn't he?" my mother would exclaim excitedly, whenever the announcer made the call and Henke trotted onto the field, looking indeed like an ungainly high-school student. "But boy, can he *pitch!*"

When Henke most decidedly did *not* throw his fastball by Jim Sundburg of the Kansas City Royals and gave up a three run triple in the sixth inning to lose the seventh and final game of the 1985 American League pennant race, she, and the rest of the country, promptly dropped him as her favourite player. But, a true baseball fan at heart, my mother stuck by the team as a whole even in the late nineties, when the back-to-back World Series titles in '92 and '93 were merely the ghost of a memory. She still insisted, whenever she came to visit, that we go and sit through another game, eat the jumbo hot dogs, giant salted pretzels, and pepperoni pizza, and drink the outrageously priced beer and Diet Coke out of plastic cups.

But the spring of 2003 was different. It was the season of SARS, and for most of the world, Toronto was about as inviting a tourist destination as Beirut or Sarajevo. My mother regrettably admitted that she did not feel safe coming to Toronto, even to see the Blue Jays. To ameliorate the effects of what was perceived as a genuine tragedy — not the death of forty-four people from a mysterious respiratory illness, but the low stadium-attendance at the opening games of her favourite team — I secretly booked three tickets to see the Blue Jays play at Yankee Stadium in New York City the week after my parents were arriving in Ottawa. This was a triple whammy: like me, my mother was a fan of the Blue Jays *and* the Yankees *and* Manhattan, in that order.

When I called my parents to tell them what I had done, they were ecstatic, even though they didn't much care for the current president of that country — George W. Bush. My parents were usually not very interested in politics. They voted, although my mother often took pleasure in declining the vote, by handing in her ballot to the electoral officials and saying, "I don't choose *any* of these bozos!" My father always voted Liberal, but rarely discussed politics outside election time. My parents are intelligent people, but like most people in the small village where I grew up they were more concerned with gas prices and property taxes than with foreign policy and terrorism. They were hardly Greenpeace activists. Until the Bush junta made such a big deal out of it by refusing to sign, they thought the Kyoto accord was a type of Japanese car. They didn't recycle until it became law in Nova Scotia, and for a year after the municipality introduced green boxes and compost bins my mother complained about it. They used cleaning products that were immensely harmful to the ozone layer. My mother lived for Costco and Wal-Mart, and when I went home one Christmas and refused to shop there because, I complained, both US chains were ruining independent stores and local businesses in Canada, she looked at me as if I had two heads.

"Suit yourself," she said, and left me in the car while she and her sisters rushed around the aisles looking for all the latest deals and lowest prices, exclaiming in the car on the way home over the money they'd saved. For dinner, we went to Swiss Chalet, and packed what we couldn't eat in styrofoam boxes to take back for my father. We drove home in a big gas-guzzling SUV, and, once there, burned oil in the furnace that belched out heavy, black smoke from the chimney into the once bracingly clean Nova Scotia air. They had never, to my knowledge, boycotted anything or anyone in their lives.

Which was why I was so surprised when, on the day the United States unilaterally declared war on Iraq, my mother called me up and said that she and my father were not going to the Yankees-Blue Jays game in New York. Their primary concern was, of course, terrorism. As Toronto and SARS, New York City had been transformed by the events of September 11th for people in Nova Scotia into a dangerous and unpredictable place.

"But what about the tickets?" I asked her. They had cost three hundred American dollars, and I was sure that this alone would persuade her to change her mind. As Wal-Mart could testify, my mother hated above all things to waste money.

"We'll split the cost," she said finally, "and we'll take the loss."

Unlike my parents, I was not fearful of an attack on Yankee stadium or at our hotel next to Grand Central Station. I should have refused to go myself on political grounds, but I dearly loved New York, and for a number of years I had been dreaming of visiting there with my parents. The major problems of the world may in fact boil down to this — that we are so willing to sacrifice, as I was, our own principles and beliefs in order to fulfill our personal desires. At least my parents had a good, fear-based reason for not wanting to go to New York, just as they had not wanted to go to Toronto.

So they came to Ottawa as planned, and we ended up driving to Montreal to see the Expos at Olympic stadium, for what would turn out to be the first game of their penultimate season in Quebec. The Expos won against the Atlanta Braves, with a surprising attendance of over 40,000 people. Toronto often got this many for end-of-season games with pennant hopes as remote as the moons of Jupiter. It was a good game for the Expos (I had last seen them two years ago lose a bruising 16 o game to Atlanta).

The greatest excitement of the evening was caused by a staged protest held in the seventh-inning stretch. Two young men ran around the stadium on the fenced track that separates the bleachers from the diamond, the first of them holding high a pole from which flew a green-white-and-red striped flag with a yellow star in the upper left corner and an armed guerrilla-type figure painted in its centre. My mother surmised that this must be the flag of the FLQ, the Front de Libération du Québec. She was almost right. It was, in fact, the flag of the even more extremist MNLQ (Mouvement National de Libération du Québec) founded by the ex-leader of the Algeria faction of the FLQ. A murmur of dissent from the crowd in the stadium swelled, by the time the two protesters had come full circle, into a deafening chorus of boos. The biggest surprise to me was not only that all of baseball-watching Montreal were now booing the MNLQ, but that my mother and father were booing heartily and enthusiastically along with them. Afterwards, at the restaurant near our hotel, when we discussed their response to the MNLQ demonstration and terrorism and the invasion of Baghdad, my mother told me the main reason they didn't go to the Yankees-Blue Jays game was politics.

"I thought," I said, "that you didn't want to go because you thought terrorists might try and blow up Yankee Stadium?"

"That was part of it," she admitted. "But we were just as worried that we would never be able to step foot in that country again, at least not while that man is in power. Your father and I chose not to go on *moral* grounds."

The worst thing, added my father, who practised a quiet, non-restrictive Baptist faith, was that Bush called himself a Christian, which, in his words, was like a spider calling himself a fly. "That man could piss Jesus off," he said with a grimace. I sat and stared at them across the table — my normally apolitical, sedentary, ill-informed, sixty-year-old parents suddenly transformed in my eyes. Out of their capitalist-consumer backgrounds they had somehow been turned into aging activists — social advocates for change in a world they now recognized as unjust, even if they couldn't say exactly how. We finished our meal, stayed that night at the hotel, and the next day drove back to Ottawa. A few days later my parents flew back to Halifax. Several months later, when the SARS crisis was over, I moved to Toronto, which pleased my mother immensely since it meant we would need to take only a five-minute subway ride rather than a five-hour car ride to see her favourite team when she next came to visit in the spring. Our shared dream of seeing the Blue Jays play at Yankee stadium remains a dream. Neither my parents nor I have stepped foot in the United States since the invasion of Iraq.

LAMENT FOR
NEW YORK

Two weeks before the attacks on the twin towers in New York City, when Osama Bin Laden et al. raised the price of international air travel forever, I decided to drive down to Manhattan from Ottawa one Saturday afternoon, entirely on a whim. Such shenanigans, as my mother calls them, are not entirely unheard of for me. I have a manic personality, and I often make extravagant last-minute decisions. I once bought a new car without more than a half-day's consideration, and put an internet bid at Sothebys.com on an original colour-pencil sketch by Mark Rothko for $17,000 (which thankfully I didn't win). Manhattan was, I argued with myself, only eight hours away by car. I had a little extra money, nothing much to do with my weekend, and I was bored with Ottawa. I packed a bag, watered and fed the cats, secured a friend to check on them while I was gone, jumped back in my Hyundai and was off.

I had been to New York only once before, when I stopped for a night when driving down to see a friend in Sante Fe, New Mexico in January of 1998. Ever since that one night, three years before, I had been aching to go back, but had never got the chance until it occurred to me just to go and to hell with the consequences. Raised on a steady diet of American movies, television and *New York Times* best selling novels, I thought of America as a land that had been highly successful in promulgating its own mythology to the world. Driving through Saskatchewan or Manitoba, parts of my own country, I would be unlikely to recognize half of what I saw. But in New York, part of a foreign country, I recognized the name of practically every street and district. New York is the jewel in America's mythological crown. Other than Venice, it is the only city in the world that lives up to its own legend in absolutely every particular, from the awe-inspiring neon spectacle of Times Square to the marquees of Broadway and the towering, art-deco skyscrapers of lower Manhattan.

In the northern part of New York state, when my initial road-trip elation had worn off, I started to worry where I would stay when I reached the city, so I stopped and booked a hotel through a telephone booking service. It was high season, and the only room I could get was the Clarion on Park Avenue at $450 US a night. For two nights, that was well over $1,000 Canadian, but I thought *What the hell.* (Part of my problem when I make these sudden and sometimes irrational decisions is an inability to show good judgment and financial acumen.)

I got to New York after midnight, checked into my room, and spent the next two days exploring the city. I visited Times Square, Broadway, and Wall Street. I had lunch on Mott Street in China-town, an afternoon snack in a Jewish delicatessen on Second Avenue in the Lower East Side that served the best pickles and coleslaw I have ever eaten, and had dinner at a café in Soho. I didn't visit any museums or indoor cultural highlights, or even rocket to the top of the Empire State Building. I had only two days. It wasn't the usual tourist havens I was interested in. I wanted the feel of New York City — the crowds and traffic and energy. I wanted to sense its grandeur and scale. I visited the Dakota on West 87th Street, where John Lennon was murdered twenty-one years before, and sat on the benches around the IMAGINE monument Yoko Ono had placed across the street in one isolated corner of Central Park. Sunday night I went to a gay bar and danced. Afterwards I went strolling in the financial district. | 59

I ended up in Washington Square next to the sleek gigantic lighted towers of the World Trade Center. I have been a big-building freak since I was a small child, likely because in my tiny village of 80 people the tallest building was the Freeman House, a three-storey, turn-of-the-century Victorian mansion that sat at the corner of Church and School Streets until it was torn down in 1987. In my travels, I had stood before many of the tall buildings of the world — the Bank of China building in Hong Kong, the Petronas Towers in Kuala Lampur, Canary Wharf in London. To me, sky-scrapers are the great architectural achievements of our time — "the cathedrals of the twentieth century," as some anonymous admirer once dubbed them. I knew that many New Yorkers hated the World Trade towers. They thought the buildings were ugly and unusually plain, jutting up like two grey milk-cartons above the rest of Manhattan's shorter but more interesting architecture. I could not agree. I marvelled at what an engineering wonder they were; how at a certain point, as I followed the line of the buildings upward with my eye, my mind refused to register the individual floors and could only take in the lighted towers as a whole, as if they existed in an architectural dream. Little did I know, as I stood by myself in the park at two o'clock in the morning, that this would be the last time I would see them. Less than two weeks later they would be down. When I first heard what had happened, it was the towers themselves that I mourned, before the human cost could even be counted.

* * *

60 | On the morning of September 11th, I was, as usual, at my computer, working without the distractions of radio, television, or Internet, and so I did not know what was happening in my favourite city until my mother called me at noon from Nova Scotia to tell me. Like the rest of the world, I did not get any more work done that day or the next, and my perceptions of the world and politics underwent a profound shift that has never been quite righted.

My first thought, expressed to my then-boyfriend in Winnipeg (and with whom I had been having a long distance relationship for over a year), was about the new novel, which I had just finished. In a few short hours the world had changed so much that I wondered if the issues with which the book dealt were even relevant now.

My second thought was for my planned trip to New York with my boyfriend, which we had scheduled for the early part of October. We had already booked our room, to avoid the $1,000 excesses of my previous trip. In the aftermath of what Gore Vidal has called Black Tuesday, we cancelled our trip, then rescheduled it a few weeks later. In Montreal, where we were to meet before driving to Manhattan, a stranger at the airport told us that anthrax had just been delivered to the NBC building in Times Square. "It's a scare tactic," he said jauntily. "No need to be afraid."

David and I sat in the Hyundai outside the terminal and discussed it. I didn't know anything about anthrax, but David did. "Bacterial," he said. "Contagious, but not airborne. We'll be fine." (We hadn't yet heard about weapons-grade anthrax.)

We decided to go. We got caught in the Montreal traffic, drove for six hours, and ended up in Manhattan at midnight. We were staying at a dive on 22nd Street, off Eighth Avenue, in the village. David had never been there, and as I am a great believer in first impressions, I took him through Times Square to our hotel on the Lower West Side. But the place was deserted. The anthrax had scared people more than the radio newscasters had let on. The sausage-and-pretzel vendors were still there (like cockroaches, they will survive any catastrophe), but had few customers. Only a few young kids, a cop, the occasional tourist, and the giant TV screens and walls of blinking neon advertising to no one could be found in the broad, deserted expanse of the square and the empty avenues and streets beyond.

To this day, the shock of seeing Times Square like this has not left me. The next morning the New York Times carried a story about weapons-grade anthrax and the estimated numbers of dead it could cause were it to be released in the ventilation system of the subway. (No mention was made of the fact that this had been tried a few years before by the Aum Shinriky cult in Japan, to no avail.) I was terrified, afraid to go out at all. David saw the articles for what they were — hysterical and reactionary. He sat me down over breakfast and tried to reason with me.

"Did it ever occur to you that it might be possible for whoever fetches you that orange juice to pour poison in it?"

"No, I never thought of that," I said. "Thanks loads for bringing it up."

"I'm serious," he said. "If you go to a restaurant, there's nothing you can do to stop someone in the kitchen from poisoning your juice, or your food. If you think about that all the time, you'll stop enjoying restaurants. You might even stop going to them. So think of life as a restaurant, and everyone in that restaurant as vulnerable. Don't stop enjoying yourself because the potential for disaster is all around you. It always has been around you, and these media assholes only want you to keep reading by making you paralyzed by it. So let's go out and enjoy the city while we're here."

That may be some of the best advice I have ever received in my life. We went out and had a good day. I tried not to think about the possibility of biological attack. I took David to all my favourite haunts, and he dragged me to a few places I would never have gone otherwise — like the top of the Empire State Building and a Buddhist temple on Mott Street. We took the *A* Train to Harlem. (David, a musician, hummed the jazz tune of the same name the entire way.) A homeless black man got on at 94th Street and started prophesying doomsday and the end of the world. (At home, in Nova Scotia, on this same day, an aunt called my mother in hysterics, predicting the same thing.) A young woman with a child on her lap screamed at the man to be quiet, that he was scaring the child, though anyone could see it was she that was frightened.

On 128th Street, renamed a few years ago after Martin Luther King Jr., we walked behind a black man and woman talking about September 11th. Downtown, everyone had American flags hanging from their apartment balconies and flying from the windows of their cars. Opinion was united. But in Harlem, as it had been for a hundred years or more, things were not so simple.

"Terrorism?" the woman was saying. "You want terrorism? What about what the whites did to the Indians in this country. Put 'em on reservations. And what about what they did to us? Slavery and lynching and shoving us down in the ghettos? I'll show you terrorism. This fucking country was *built* on terrorism!"

It was as if we were living in a dream, or a nightmare. New York had·changed from just a few weeks before. Uptown was angry. Midtown was empty. Downtown was shocked and battered and spookily quiet. Many of the streets in lower Manhattan were blocked off while the cleanup continued. Later in the day back downtown, David and I stood at an intersection waiting to cross the street, when a flatbed rumbled by carrying a sixty-foot metal beam pulled from the wreckage of the towers. The beam was blackened and twisted from the pressure and the heat. A man in an expensive three-piece suit waiting for the light beside us shook his head, looked at the beam then at us, and said, "Holy fucking Christ!"

A month after the disaster, and the entire city still reeked of smoke, charred plastic, and some unnameable chemical odour that stung the eyes and burned the nostrils like cordite. There were few tourists. We ran into two middle-aged women from Colorado who had come to show their support for the city, as we had. On top of the Empire State Building, we saw a commercial jet charting a course over the harbour, and everyone, as soon as they heard it, turned towards the plane and froze. What September 11th had done, beyond instill fear into a continent that had known little of it over the centuries, was make us aware of our own vulnerability. For the first time, the waiter had poured poison into the orange juice, and none of us — not myself, not the man standing at the corner, not David or my mother or my aunt, would ever trust the staff, or the owners, or the restaurant, or perhaps anyone, again.

* * *

My mother used to say that for every negative there is a positive: put in terms of Newtonian physics, for every action there is an equal and opposite reaction. The immediate reaction to September 11th by the people of the city of New York was shock and fear. But there was another subtle shift in the public mood. Osama Bin Laden did what millions of dollars of TV promotion and a mayor who understood the vital importance of tourism on the Manhattan economy could not: he rendered New Yorkers, in the short term at least, emotionally tractable. The traditional New York gruffness had given way to an almost desperate gratitude that we had braved the anthrax scare and the smoking ruins of the towers to spend our time and money there. Banks didn't charge us for changing over traveller's cheques. Restaurants gave us free coffee; the hotel lowered its price by half, even after we took the room at the original cost. David, being a pianist, always had to be doing something with his fingers, so he carried with him a long piece of string tied end-to-end and on the subway he made cat's cradles and other elaborate designs while we rocketed along underneath the city. He had been practising this art for years, and was an expert at it. He made bears and turtles and lions and cars and triangles within circles within squares. He often caught the attention of those sitting around us; his "incredible walking duck" always got at least a smile out of the most uptight subway-going Manhattanites. From Christopher Street up to 87th Street he entertained a black woman and her four kids with a dazzling array of string animals, wrought quickly one after the other and then banished with a flick of his wrist; soon everyone on the car was watching and applauding after each execution. It restored my faith in the world a little bit, and in art — the power of art, even silly, stupid string art, to unite us and make us forget our horrors for a while.

In Central Park, two American soldiers on leave — but still in uniform — tramped unthinkingly over Lennon's monument: the smooth, round flagstone with *IMAGINE* engraved upon it that Yoko had sunk evenly into the earth as a tribute to her dead husband. The irony of the soldiers marching over the stone was not lost on David, nor on me, nor on any of the other Lennon fans sitting around, meditating and paying homage to the great singer and his vision of world peace.

It was a sign of things to come.

The night before we left New York we went to Charlie Parker's Birdland Jazz Bar for dinner. On the way home, outside the YMCA on Eighth Avenue and 26th Street, we came across a dead man on the sidewalk. The police and paramedics were just arriving. The body had not been covered with a blanket. It looked like he had been shot, judging by the amount of blood spreading slowly out over the concrete.

I don't think I will ever forget that dead, mangled body, and how I was filled once more with both the horror of what had just happened in the city and the world and also with a kind of nameless, burgeoning hope. It was as if, for me at least, the dead body symbolized a moving on, that New York was getting back to its daily preoccupations of violence and prodigious self-absorption, instead of the eerie, solemn weirdness of the previous two days. Someone had killed someone. No surprise, in such a place. And the police could get on with the task of trying to figure out why, and how, and who. Regular people would gawk, and shake their heads, and secretly be thrilled at witnessing such an event. At last, New York was again living up to its own myth.

The next day David and I went home.

Since the US declared war on Iraq, I have not stepped foot into the United States. I miss New York. I miss Chinatown, Christopher Street, Central Park. I miss walking in the shadows of the great buildings, along the broad avenues, poking through the nooks and crannies and alleyways and side streets of the great, unsolvable concrete maze. I miss the way the snow falls in Manhattan, as it did the first time I was there, and how the city, always so vibrant and noisy and alive, is somehow transformed, becomes muted and serene — almost peaceful. I even miss the two lighted towers, and standing at their feet in the park in the dead of night. But most of all, I miss those naive and innocent days before the towers fell, those days before I realized that the dream of our prosperity was over, our security an illusion, our immortality a comforting myth that could be ripped from us like a blanket by a stranger in the middle of the night.

FIVE
GENERATIONS

In the summer of 2000 I was lucky enough to travel to South Africa for the first time. I'd been to the continent once before, when I took a ferry from Algeciras, Spain to Tangiers for an afternoon. Once there, hounded by spice merchants while being led hurriedly through the labyrinth streets of the Casbah by our guide, a short Moroccan man whose estimation of the best attraction of Morocco was his cousin's overpriced carpet-shop. But South Africa, I imagined, would be different. I had read Dinisen's *Out Of Africa* and Hemingway's *The Snows of Kilimanjaro*. Never mind that these stories were set in Kenya and what would become Tanzania. With my typical North American ignorance of geography, I thought I could jump on a train that would take me from Durban to Nairobi in a few hours, rather than the three days it actually takes: a fact I found out when I arrived.

I'm not exactly sure what I expected when I arrived in South Africa, perhaps a lioness ready to spring out at me as we disembarked from the plane onto the tarmac at the airport in Durban, but I remember feeling slightly disappointed that it looked like any airport anywhere. Even the row of singing and dancing Zulu men in traditional costume, waiting for us in the hangar, didn't do much to cheer me up; they were, after all, in an airplane hangar waiting for tourists, and probably getting paid for their trouble. What I wanted, I think now, was the genuine article: for South Africa to ignore me and at the same time to lay out at my feet all her treasures of culture and wildlife and landscape and legendary extremes. I got what I wanted, I suppose. I did see what I consider to be the most beautiful tree in the world, the acacia, almost as soon as I left the airport, and seeing a giraffe and elephant up close on safari was a boy's dream made manifest. I swam in the Indian Ocean at midnight off the boardwalk in Durban, in the warmest water I have ever felt, and I haggled for Zulu masks in the markets with an old woman who kissed the rand I gave her and hid it away in the folds of her apron when she thought I wasn't looking. These are not the things I will remember from my journey there when I am old and grey and I recount these adventures of mine to some uninterested relative who listens because I buy nice gifts. Perhaps it is my personality (I have been accused before of being a glass-half-full kind of guy), but what I will remember will be the shocking vision of a country trying to right itself, to cast off the legacy of its old racist regime. Above all, I noticed the people.

II

The situation of the African people in South Africa, what I saw of it, reminded me of the stories and plays and television shows I've read or seen about the situation of African Americans in the

American South after the abolition of slavery in 1865 and before the American civil-rights uprisings in the 1960s.

Each morning I would get up early and wait for the first bus to arrive at the University of Natal, where I was put up for the week, to take me to downtown Durban for the day. Always, another bus would arrive at the stop five minutes before mine and disgorge a small army of black women, dressed in blue cotton outfits, with kerchiefs wrapped about their heads, lugging cloths and mops and pails up the remainder of the hill to the university residence. Although I'm certain these women were paid (according to one reporter on gay.com, they received about three rand, or seventy-five cents, a day), the scene struck me as being reminiscent of the days of slavery. It wasn't just the cliché Aunt Jemima outfits, all disturbingly identical in colour and make, as if they had been commissioned, but it was the expressions these women wore. It was a heavy look — tired, burdened, resentful, yet cautiously neutral — a look described many times in books I have read. It is the look of the African American in the pre-civil rights South, of the East Timorese in Indonesia, the Jews in Nazi-occupied Germany, and North American Aboriginal people on reservations and residential schools for many hundreds of years here in Canada. In short, I saw on the faces of those women the look of the hopelessly oppressed.

There were other instances, too, that made me feel as if I had been transported back into some dreadful time in North America's past. A group of us from Canada had planned a safari for one of the days of the conference, and I had to go down to the bus stop even earlier that day, at dawn, to wait for the safari shuttle to take me to a downtown hotel. The shuttle was late (in fact, it never showed at all and I had to take a taxi), and I had lots of time to sit around on a bench and watch Durban wake up.

A large truck trundled slowly by at one point with the name of some Durban-based construction company decaled on its side; crowded on the flatbed were fifty or so black men, in blue overalls, being transported like cattle out of the city for a day's work on the highways. I was to see this over and over again that day — small groups of black men in these identical blue overalls shovelling dirt and black-topping the roads as we drove through the countryside to Umfolozi National Park. Different men, in the same blue outfits, stood in the fields with machetes, hacking away under the hot African sun at stalks of ripe sugar cane.

I was told that whites still own the construction companies, the sugar cane plantations, and the refineries. These workers were getting paid, of course, but so were the blacks in the South after the American Civil War. Of course, they were no longer housed, or fed, and the wages were scaled down enough to make their economic situations no better than they had been when they received no money at all. In South Africa the dynamic was slightly different.

Blacks were always paid, but they had to live in certain places ("homelands," in the wildly inaccurate and racist-romantic language of the apartheid Afrikaner). They had many restrictions placed on their movements and lives. Now, nominally, they have their freedom. But is it freedom when you all dress the same, are paid next to nothing, own little, are hungry in the streets built by whites that now, at least nominally, are your own? I don't think I will ever forget the maids at the hotel, or the men on their way in the flat beds to the cut sugar cane or work on the roads.

And all this without mentioning AIDS at all. Over four million people in South Africa are infected with HIV — the second highest rate of infection in the world. According to one statistic that I heard, a person dies from an AIDS-related illness in the country every two minutes. And according to a source I read, if the tide of HIV infection continues, as many as five countries in Africa could economically collapse within the next eight years — including the country I visited. Freedom has a long way to go yet before it arrives in South Africa.

|71

III

A friend of mine believes it takes five generations for a system that has been thrown out of balance through oppression to right itself. Five generations before the blacks in South Africa can get back on their feet, overcome the economic apartheid still thriving there, and at last become able to call their country their own and earn their living the way they choose. Five generations, by my calculations, is 100 years — about the amount of time that elapsed between the abolition of slavery in the US and the first galvanizing civil-rights protest by Rosa Parks in Alabama in 1955. My hope is that the five generational rule, if something so vague can be called a rule, can be shortened in South Africa and in countries like it. Yet, as much as I would like that to happen, I doubt it will.

Occasionally, as we were driving in our air-conditioned bus to Umfolozi, we would pass roadside villages — a collection of squalid corrugated-tin or grass huts, with a chicken or two, if the occupants were lucky, strutting in the yard. We've all seen photographs of the two sides of Africa we've imagined: the rolling savannah teeming with exotic wildlife — tigers and lions and elephants; and the abject poverty — a critically thin black woman standing in the doorway of her hut clutching an equally thin child with distended stomach, both of them looking out with pleading expressions and haunting, sunken eyes. Both are exaggerations. The parks are not teeming with wildlife — you have to look hard to see anything. The herds of wildebeest and zebra, if you're lucky, are twenty or so in number. The images of starving people are from UNICEF photographs taken during a famine. There is no famine in South Africa right now, unless it be a famine of economic equality, what I believe to be a famine of economic human rights.

Often the bus would have to stop for construction on the roads, and the children from the villages would run up to the windows of the bus and hold up fruit for us to buy. I bought, over the course of the day, a bag of oranges, a two rand bunch of bananas, two pineapples, and about a half-dozen avocados. I had no use for the avocados. I don't even like them. But the avocado girl outside my window was having no luck selling them, so I thought, *What the hell, it's only a dollar.* Most of this food I took back to the university, laid it out on a towel on my bed, and just admired it as if I were an artist contemplating the production of a still life.

I feel guilty still. I should have just given the money — thrown rand out the window like the rich tourist I was perceived to be. These children weren't starving. (If they were, they could have eaten the pineapples they sold us.) But for these children, living with no running water in little huts, selling fruits to passing busloads of tourists, starvation couldn't be very far away. All it would take is a drought, another civil war, an economic sanction or two, and these children could be there.

And even if all went well with the country and the rainy season, being able to eat fruit is not enough. Mark Kingwell, the University of Toronto philosopher and author of the book *Better Living: In Pursuit of Happiness from Plato to Prozac*, states that poverty is relative anyway, a matter of perception rather than reality. What we consider poor today might not have been considered poor five | 73 hundred or even a hundred years ago. It's no longer enough to provide someone with the basics of living (if you consider the lack of access to HIV medications in South Africa, we're not even doing that). We need to provide each other with the things that allow us to participate fully in the world we have created. That means technology, education, and materials other than the ones you can eat and build with. We need to give South Africans the means of communicating with the rest of the world. Deny someone a voice and you kill them as surely as if you deny them food.

At the very least, as the world is now learning, you drive them to be heard in other ways, such as committing great acts of violence — blowing themselves up in a crowded Tel Aviv market, mailing envelopes of powdered anthrax to NBC journalists and public officials, flying planes into tall Manhattan buildings.

I think now the reason I was so shocked by what I saw in South Africa was that it was my first visit to what we so arrogantly in North America call the "developing" world. Since then, I have been to many such places. I have seen the squalid, disease-plagued slums on the outskirts of Delhi, the shacks built on stilts in the parasite-infested mud of Tonlé Sap river in Cambodia, mere children selling their pre-pubescent bodies for a German mark in Bangkok. Yet, South Africa is in a way a perfect microcosm of all the systems of the world that have gone haywire, for it has both the poverty of a "third world" country and the economic infrastructure of a white, oppressive "first world" regime superimposed upon it. Unfortunately, there are no signs that the old oppressors will relinquish their economic hold any time soon.

74 | The world is slow to change. People, however, often change dramatically and suddenly. After I returned from South Africa, I took my first tentative steps toward throwing off the comforting but egregious North American perception that the world is a good, safe, and prosperous place full of good, safe, and prosperous people. I joined an activist group that lobbies for cheaper HIV medications for poorer countries, and attempted to become, in the humblest of ways, an agent for social change. This, as it turned out, was a much greater gift to me than Zulus and elephants and acacia trees and all the clichés of South Africa's glorious and turbulent past put together.

WE SHALL
OVERCOME
... MAYBE

The two of us felt like Hunter S. Thompson going to Las Vegas, without the uppers and pint of raw ether. We had Pete Seeger playing on the car stereo. We had also brought along CDs of the Beatles, Bob Dylan, Peter, Paul and Mary, and the soundtrack of *Hair*. Secretly, I had visions of getting everyone to sing "We Shall Overcome" or "Guantanamera" outside the wall of the Summit.

Five and a half hours to drive to Quebec from Ottawa on the last day of the People's Summit. It was already 3:00 p.m. By the time we got there, it would likely be over anyway. But we were going. An article in the *Globe & Mail* that morning about the unconstitutional arrest of Jaggi Singh and the treatment of protestors by police had fired us up. Both of us angry, we had made the decision over brunch at Denny's that we would go. We packed a few clothes, filled up the Hyundai with gas, and hit the highway.

Once Sam mentioned gas masks, but we never followed through. I don't think either of us believed we would really need them, despite the *Globe & Mail* article. We were more concerned about seeing whether this was real or not, or maybe it was just being able to say we were there. Our spirits seemed pretty high for two guys heading into a massive anti-trade protest and its possible violence. But we were members of the Me Generation. The sixties and Vietnam were over before we developed a regular conscience, let alone a political one. We had lived through the eighties as consumers-without-a-cause, and the creeping malaise of a capitalist pseudo-democratic society in decline had been numbing our spirits and soothing our disquiet with television commercials and Wal-Mart sales for decades. Finally, we had an enemy: the great corporate/government/globalization evil alliance.

It was the rebels against the Imperialist alliance. It was Frodo and the Fellowship against the evil armies of Sauron. It was Kent State and Tiananmen Square rolled up into one. At the risk of sounding cynical: not quite.

* * *

One of the great problems with the anti-globalization movement has been, it seems to me, a desperate lack of leadership. On the one hand you have the non-governmental organizational elite fighting for specific issues, such as access to medications, reduction of Third World debt, environmental protectionism, the banning of genetically modified foods, and intellectual property rights. On the other, you have the great, wide, eternally dissatisfied sea of youth who know something is wrong with the world but can't exactly put their fingers on what the problem is, or what to do about it. These are the minions who show up to protests in army jackets and Doc Martin boots, with colourful pieces of cloth wrapped about their heads. Corn-fed young men and women with bees in their bandanas about the state of the world and looking for someone to blame it on.

They could do worse than to start with the corporations. Robert Kaplan, the American foreign policy analyst and essayist, says that global corporations do commit their fair share of atrocities and abuses. He also says these companies get away with it because they are thinking on a global scale, viewing all the world as a relatively homogeneous market, whereas the governments that are meant to make them accountable are still thinking in a provincial, nationalistic way. In his book *The Coming Anarchy*, he says that governments and the people who elect them will, in the long run, be forced to catch up, to think of the world as one community, in order to put the corporations back under their control. It's possible that the protests may accomplish this, but not with the current strategy. The intellectual elite who face down the corporations every day on these issues tend to distance themselves from the masses of protesters such as those who showed up in Quebec.

No wonder.

When Sam and I arrived there, we found nothing but chaos.

To begin with, we drove right into a tear-gas attack in the lower city. We were forced to abandon the car in the middle of the street, and ran away from the advancing wall of gas with our hands over our noses and mouths. We found sanctuary half a mile up the road, in a café. Later, a couple of protesters lent us their gas masks so that we could go back and get the car and safely park it miles away from the walls of the old city.

It was about six o'clock in the evening by then, and much of the gas had cleared, though enough of it hung in the air to sting our eyes and form a dense fog everywhere we went. Along the way we found a middle-aged woman dressed in faded jeans and a tie-dyed

T-shirt and dirty bandana — clearly a hold-over from the sixties — sitting on the curb and sobbing.

"What's wrong?" Sam asked her.

"This is not the world I was born into," she told us.

Sam and I helped her up and sent her out of the gas zone before we retrieved the car and returned the masks to the men who had lent them to us. We were a bit embarrassed at not having brought masks ourselves.

"Try a bandana soaked in vinegar held over your mouth and nose," the men with the masks told us. "That'll do in a pinch."

But there were no more gas attacks that evening. After awhile, we got the courage to go up Laurier Avenue next to the Plains of Abraham, where the gates had come down during the riots the day before and where Jaggi Singh had been arrested. There we found the entrance to the Summit protected by impenetrable lines of police in full riot gear, banging on their Plexiglas shields with their billy clubs and looking like the storm troopers out of *Star Wars* or like the lines of guards at the Nuremberg rallies in Leni Riefenstahl's *Triumph of the Will*. Facing them were the unruly masses, thousands of young men and women milling about the streets, unsure of what to do next.

The overall mood was calm compared to what it must have been the day before, or even earlier than afternoon when they released the teargas. It had grown dark; a few dozen people were sitting down in the street trying to figure out what to do. Sam and I, spectators to the end, sat down with them and listened. In turn, each person stood up and made a case for action.

"We should move up closer to the gates and sit-in," said one person.

"We should just stay here," said another.

"We should all keep our cell phones on and use them to communicate," suggested one more. "That way we could storm the gates on several fronts at once."

In the midst of all this, members of the Black Bloc, the Quebec anarchist group, circled the sit-in and cried out that there were police in riot gear descending upon us from the side streets and that we should stand up and fight. Fighting a growing sense of panic, Sam whispered to me that we should get out of here before they arrived and we got thrown in jail, or worse, got the Jaggi Singh treatment.

"No," I said. "I want to stay."

I was feeling that sense of solidarity, of being, for the first time in my life, a part of a just cause in opposition to a ruling and unjust power.

Except the feeling would be short-lived. It turned out there were no advancing battalions in riot gear. That was a lie spread by the Black Bloc to incite us to violence, to fulfill their own agenda. Among the hundred or so people sitting on the street, consensus could not be reached. One person put it best. "We either do it together, or not at all."

I never saw his face, but he had it right. Leadership is not one person standing in front of others telling them what to do: it's one person or a few people making sure that whatever action is taken, it is taken in concert.

Some from the group ignored the consensus process and went marching up to the front lines of policemen, shouting out rallying calls to get others to follow. There was screaming and shouting and acrimony among the group. About a third of the group followed the breakaway members and the rest stayed. The breakaway group eventually broke up again when they couldn't decide what to do once they got up to the gate and faced the lines of formidable policemen. One of the leaders of this new rebel alliance shouted out to the few who were leaving, "You're a part of the problem! You're the fucking enemy!"

And yet, I knew, and Sam knew, perhaps from having a few more years experience on the earth, that once you break consensus and walk away you open the doors for consensus to be broken again, and some of those in your group will eventually walk away from you, led by your previous example. Revolution begets revolution, even among revolutionaries. At that moment, the battle of the dissatisfied youth of the world against the global corporate alliance was lost, though the war is still being fought on many other, less conspicuous, fronts.

* * *

At the Ottawa International Writers' Festival in 2003, John Ralston Saul said that perhaps the biggest effect of September 11th is that it belied the fact that the world operates solely on the principle of self-interest — free-market, competition, everyone for themselves — which has so long been the tune sung by the capitalist choir. Those initial days in the aftermath of the tragedy, Saul said, amidst all the hype and the maudlin sentiment and the propaganda, were filled with examples of people caring for people in times of crisis, and countries caring for countries.

But, said Saul, September 11th also proved beyond a doubt the limitations of corporations, and showed their inability to act in the face of world crisis. When the crunch came, it was *nations* that had to step forward once again and take control. The companies, whose only purpose is to make money for their shareholders, had to take a back seat. Perhaps this is the reason why the majority of protests that have taken place since then have been against the resurgence of a rabidly nationalist America, with its regime trying to stamp out security threats, both real and imagined, and thus creating an army of new threats for us to deal with in the process.

A few friends of mine still believe in the anti-corporation movement, which reached its apex in Seattle in 2000. They continue to organize sit-ins and teach-ins and such. But the crowds that showed up in Quebec no longer exist. The fashion of the day has moved on, for in the end, that is what it was — a fashion.

Most of the kids who came to those rallies and protests had not felt the negative effects of globalization. They were well fed, well schooled, destined for decent lives and decent jobs. Their protests were a right of passage. A good majority of them carried around beer bottles and smoked joints while they protested, hardly a sign of earnestness and commitment. And, despite the worthiness of their cause — I heard one young man shouting out to the rows of shielded and helmeted policeman in Quebec: "Half the world's organisms are extinct, and the other half are dying!" — they will not be the ones to change the world.

Perhaps September 11th, once the dust has settled and everyone sees it in perspective, will teach us that we must advance our economies at the same rate as our democratic and political systems. Let us hope that day will come and that eventually we will learn we are interdependent: every decision made affects everyone on the planet.

ELUGELAB: CANARIES IN THE MINDSHAFT OF THE WORLD

On November 1, 1952, the first hydrogen bomb was tested by the United States on the tiny atoll of Elugelab in the Pacific Ocean. The bomb was designed by the Hungarian-born physicist Edward Teller. He was inspired by the Italian physicist Enrico Fermi (1901–1954), who had proposed the possibility of a hydrogen bomb during a lunch between the two physicists when they worked together on the Manhattan Project some years before. Fermi and Oppenheimer and some of the other atomic physicists refused to work on the A-bomb and left the project after the end of the Second World War.

Teller stayed. His goal was to create — à la Fermi — a bomb that would not just split atoms and release energy like the atomic bomb dropped in Japan seven years earlier, but one that would fuse deuterium, tritium, and hydrogen isotopes in a chemical reaction similar to that which takes place in the core of the sun. The H-bomb initiates an atomic fission (splitting) reaction, which is followed by a fusion reaction that releases heat and energy — the explosion — in amounts up to 100 times greater than those from the atomic bomb.

Quite an advancement.

Unless of course you happen to live on the tiny island of Elugelab in the Pacific Ocean.

* * *

In 1952 I was not yet born. My father was twelve, my mother, thirteen, and they had not yet met each other. When they did meet, in 1966, the Cold War was in full swing. Kubric had filmed Dr. Strangelove in 1964 (the title character of which was based on Edward Teller). It's a nuclear satire, aptly subtitled: How I Learned to Stop Worrying and Love the Bomb. By the time the film was made, most everyone had become used to living under the constant threat of a nuclear holocaust.

By the time I was born in 1968, there was nothing special or unusual or more than occasionally frightening about a bomb that could release the equivalent of 100 million tons of TNT in one shot. Neville Shute had already published *On the Beach*, a novel about the destruction of the world by nuclear war and about its survivors, who were waiting out the end of their lives in Australia. "Nuclear deterrence" was a commonly accepted idea among politicians and average citizens. Despite the occasional protest, people like my parents had become accustomed to the idea of this Sword of Damocles hanging over their heads. There was only one group of the citizenry (besides those pesky nuclear protestors) — thankfully a small, adult minority who were difficult to convince: for some reason, children seemed to worry a lot about nuclear war.

* * *

In university, I once asked a group of my fellow students during one of our late-night bull sessions in our dorm what they had thought of the threat of nuclear holocaust when they were young. Without exception, all of them said they went through a period when it was all they thought about. My friend Jeff told me of a time when he went to bed every night convinced that *that* was going to be the night they dropped the bomb. Once, there was a chimney fire in the house across the street from his house in Miramachi, New Brunswick, and he woke up to sirens and smoke and the glint of flame in his window. He jumped up and ran out of his room screaming and crying until his parents convinced him that it was simply a chimney fire and not the end of the world.

My own experience was no less riddled with the same kind of tension. I went through a period, from the age of about ten to fifteen, where I thought about the possibility constantly. I used to ask my teachers and my parents questions about nuclear holocaust all the time. I remember in grade eight asking my science teacher, Mr. M, how long we would have to wait before the air would be breathable and radiation-free again if they dropped a hydrogen bomb.

"Presuming," he said, "it didn't land near us and vaporize us instantly?"

"Yes," I answered. "Presuming that."

He shrugged, seemingly unconcerned about the whole thing. "Ten or twenty years in the immediate locale," he said.

I remember I felt, for the briefest of seconds, a tremendous sense of relief. Ten or twenty years underground, assuming the bomb landed far enough away, and we could crawl out again and resume our old lives again. Whew! This balloon of nascent optimism, however, had barely begun to rise when Mr. M (my own junior high school equivalent of Dr. Strangelove) pulled out his trusty intellectual pin.

"Of course," he said, "the likelihood of dropping only one bomb would be minimal. Most probably, if they were to start dropping, they would let go the entire nuclear arsenal, and very few of us would survive, even if we did manage somehow to make it underground."

86 |

"But if we did," I said, clinging desperately to my childish hope, "how long would it take before we could come out again?"

Again Mr. M shrugged. "A thousand years. Maybe longer. And when we did, nuclear winter would have killed off all life anyway and the planet would be uninhabitable. All this provided we didn't split the planet in two or knock it out of its orbit and send it flying into the sun or interstellar space."

In retrospect, in spite of bringing roaring to the surface my until-then subterranean sense of terror and fear, I am grateful to Mr. M. He was the first adult to talk to me honestly about the results of full-scale nuclear war. Everyone else tried to assuage my fears by saying it would never happen, the same way that politicians tried to assuage the fears of the public by speaking empty, sophistic words about deterrents, the necessity of first-strike capabilities, and the possibility of limited nuclear exchange. One teacher said that when I grew up I would simply stop worrying about nuclear holocaust.

"You just will learn to live with it, and go about your life despite it," this teacher blithely pronounced. I forget exactly who she was or what she looked like. In my memory she is only a presence, standing for all those supposedly rational conversations I had with grownups as a boy that make little or no sense to me even today. But to this day, I remember how powerfully these words affected me, and how even then I knew to be the truth: adult human beings can actually get used to and then start ignoring such a thing. This was more horrifying in some ways than the threat of nuclear Armageddon itself. I was too young to realize then what I know now — the two ideas were connected, indeed one would not have been possible without the other. Our genius for ignoring such |87 horrors makes them possible to begin with. It may be that our strength — the peculiarly human ability to adapt to practically any circumstance, no matter how dispiriting or even terrifying — is the cause of our enormous evolutionary success, but it could also in the end be responsible for our eventual destruction.

* * *

I first read about Elugelab in a book by Peter Watson called *A Terrible Beauty*, a history of the ideas that have shaped the modern mind. Information about the testing of the new hydrogen bomb was nothing new to me. I had read about such things before. What shocked me so was the news that the tiny island of Elugelab no longer existed. When the first hydrogen bomb exploded, the island was instantly vaporized. No one lived on the island, which is how the US government and scientists like Teller justified their actions.

Let me restate that: no *human beings* lived on the island. I'm assuming that, like all islands, the atoll was a rich ecosystem that sustained a variety of creatures, both above ground and below it and in the sea. A million gallons of ocean instantly evaporated with the heat of the bomb and, presumably, all the organic life that those million gallons contained, ranging in size from plankton to whales, went with it. All the shock and horror I felt as a kid came rushing back when I read about the missing island. All those creatures going about their lives as normal and then — zap! They were no longer. That island stands for the world in microcosm — how something that is can just be blown away by a technology that not even the scientists who invented it understand very well, beyond the purely physical mechanics of the thing. Where Elugelab once stood now remains only sea.

88 |

The threat of nuclear Armageddon, if I believe what we are told, has also evaporated. Since the 1980s, the richest countries of the world with the largest nuclear arsenals have signed stockpile reduction treaties and dismantled their bombs, while poorer countries have been busy acquiring them.

The height of the Pakistan/India nuclear crisis was the summer of 2002, when India sent one million troops to the Kashmiri border and both countries were testing bombs in their deserts. This was an indirect threat of possible action. I was in the exiled Nepalese government stronghold of McLeod Ganj, the home of the four-teenth Dalai Lama, in the Indian Himalayas. The Canadian consulate had issued warnings to Canadian citizens to leave India, as the threat of nuclear war loomed closer than it had since the Cuban Missile Crisis. I chose to stay, reasoning that travelling to Delhi, a prime target for the Pakistan military, would be foolhardy, especially with no guarantee that I would even get a flight out. I also reasoned that no country in the world (China excepted) would be stupid enough to bomb the home of the Dalai Lama, and so I decided to stay put. My hosts — two young Kashmiri men who ran the family hotel in McLeod Ganj where I was staying — promised me that if anything "bad" was to happen, they would take me with them into the mountains, and there we would hide until the fallout — political and nuclear — had played itself out.

I felt like a frightened child all over again. Here I was, in the post-Cold War, with the Berlin wall torn down, and worrying once again about being vaporized by manipulated atoms, the building blocks of our universe. Each night I sat up with my two male hosts in a glassed-in room at the top of the hotel, with a breathtaking view of the Dhauladhar mountain range and the Kangra valley five thousand feet below. We talked about war, the possibility of war, President Vajpayee, and President Musharraf, and how they were handling the crisis in Kashmir.

Like me in Grade eight, my two hosts also thought that nuclear warfare was just a larger version of conventional warfare, that it would not spell the end of their environment and their way of life. They were not alone. A national Indian radio station interviewed a hundred people on the streets in Delhi and Mumbai, two of the most likely targets if such a war were to come, and found that most had no idea what the consequences of nuclear war would be. Some of them had never even heard of radiation fallout, and what it could do to organic life.

Not that Indians are stupid. Far from it. But they had not grown up under the implied threat of the Cold War. I was experiencing — in a shortened, more intense version — what I had already lived with while I was growing up in the "duck and cover" North American atmosphere of the Cold War era.

And so, based on my experience in India (and my recently acquired knowledge that of 100 suitcase nuclear bombs built by the Soviet army during the Cold War less than a third are accounted for), I am convinced that the threat of nuclear destruction is not

89

over. All of the nuclear arsenal that existed in the 1980s during the Cold War exists today — even if some of the missiles are in pieces — and a certain number of bombs are still installed on hair-triggers.

In the case of Russia, they exist within a system of command and control forces, both mechanical and social, that are rapidly deteriorating. In 1995, a weather-rocket launched from the seas of Norway activated Boris Yeltsin's nuclear briefcase, and the Russian nuclear response team went into action, certain that the United States was firing at them. The response was shut down by a clear-headed Russian military officer only minutes before Russia's entire nuclear arsenal was launched at North America in retaliation.

George W. Bush's attempts to pass the development of "bunker buster" nuclear weapons through the US Congress is in fact an attempt to violate international arms treaties and to break the nuclear taboo that has existed since the world first realized the potential horror of nuclear destruction, when the atomic bombs were dropped on Japan.

And so here we are again. Duck and cover. Limited response. Poised once more on the brink of man-made disaster.

* * *

After the fall of the World Trade towers, I heard a report on American news that children were having a very difficult time adjusting to the new, post-September 11th reality. Many of them, so this report said, were suffering anxiety and depression about the state of the world, and I immediately thought of myself at age twelve or so, constantly worrying about a nuclear holocaust. There is a tendency (there certainly was in this news program) to dismiss the fears and anxieties of children as out of proportion to the intensity of the threat. The news reporter interviewed psychologists suggesting ways to calm kids down and assuage their fears so they could sleep at night.

While on the one hand I understand the need to comfort children, I also believe that often they are not the ones who need the therapy. Children are like the canaries in the mineshaft of our world — they can detect genuine danger long before adults have registered it, and long after their parents have calmed their own anxiety with Scotch, sitcoms, a new leather sofa and big screen TV, or an suv. | 91

Children also often have the answers about how we can get ourselves out of the mess we have created. These answers are usually dismissed by adults as, of course, obvious, naive and childish. Often they are correct. But the complex rationalizations of adults are not so easily dismissed or argued against. Those mature members of the human race are the same people who, against all evidence, have learned to live with the mess. This kind of thinking takes a long time to establish and much work to maintain; a few straightforward questions and suggestions by children to start loving one another, end poverty, give up our weapons, etc. are not going to destroy our hard-won denial.

I ran up against this for the first time in Grade eleven, when I was on a debating team in my English class. The subject was nuclear disarmament. I got to choose the side I wanted to be on, and of course I chose pro-disarmament. Another friend, and his debating partner, gladly took up anti-disarmament. We debated this topic in front of three combined classes and several teachers elected as judges for the event.

I lost the debate. It was on that day I learned that I would make a terrible lawyer. (I had toyed with the idea of law school ever since my parents implanted the idea when I was five.) Arguing against disarmament was unthinkable, and going into the debate I couldn't imagine how anyone could even consider the idea. Here we were facing the worst crisis in the history of the world and someone was going to make an argument to *keep* nuclear weapons? Absurd!

I underestimated my friend, whose name was Harold. Harold would have made an excellent lawyer, and my appeals to him and his debating partner, the audience and the judges, that we were living under the threat of total nuclear destruction, were made in vain. Coolly, and with considerable aplomb, Harvey challenged and then dismantled every one of my assumptions and proclamations.

"Who would disarm first?" Harvey asked. "If we do it, then we're exposed to threat from the Russians. If they do it, then they're exposed to threat from us."

"But I'm not talking about partial nuclear disarmament!" I cried in a voice strangled by emotion, so passionately did I believe in my subject. "I'm talking about everyone disarming, and now! Immediately, before we destroy all life on our planet!"

"And how would we achieve that?" Harvey asked, smiling slightly with goodnatured contempt for my naiveté. "And even if we did disarm — us and the Russians — then the Chinese would be in control, and threaten to blow us all up and take over the world. Or the French. Disarmament is not only undesirable, it's impossible. It can never happen, so there's no use even discussing it."

By the end of this debate, I was so wound up I could barely speak straight, and friends of mine in the audience told me afterward they were embarrassed for me. For weeks I wouldn't speak to Harvey, who eventually told me, when we did start speaking again, that he didn't much care what side he was on. He liked debating, he was good at it, and he said he would have won if he had taken the pro-disarmament side. I learned the hard way — in public — that contests are awarded and decisions made on the merits of a coolly logical and dispassionately presented argument, rather than on basic common sense; that relativism and rhetoric will win the day over some objectively felt truth every time; that, indeed, those of us passionately committed to a cause often do not make good cases for that cause; and that our passion often gets in the way, so that by the end of the discussion we are left sputtering in an inarticulate rage or frustration. Lawyers and politicians, on the other hand, who are not arguing on principle but rather as a means to an end (to win a case, to win votes, to maintain the status quo), will often make a better presentation, and appeal to their audience precisely because they don't care very much about their subject.

It was a bitter pill to swallow. For years I wondered what Harvey truly believed in, beyond his passion for debating and his even-handed logic. Was he for or against? What did he believe? I could never get an answer from him, and to this day I still don't know. I suspect that Harold, and people like him, don't think much about it unless they are forced to. They have learned to live with it, but for others of us — mostly children and a few unstable adults — the anxiety and the worry is always there. The children grow up, and the adults either find outlets for their anxiety (through activism or art or both) or they end up in asylums or drunk on the street somewhere. Artists are also canaries in the mineshaft of the world — they, we, are people who have never learned to express in socially acceptable ways our anxiety for the state of the world.

So here I am, at thirty-seven years of age, and my teacher's prediction has, thankfully, not come true. I have never learned, for better or for worse, to live with things simply as they are. I am still that hopelessly inarticulate, socially awkward boy, standing up in front of my audience and crying out for everyone to listen, for everyone to open their eyes and try just for a minute to honestly and truly see.

REVELATION
IN VENICE

I was standing in the Piazza San Marco in Venice listening to a quintet flawlessly play Vivaldi along the outer gallery. I was with an elderly couple from Brazil whom I had met in the water taxi coming from the airport the day before. They were both doctors — he an obstetrician, she an ophthalmologist — and they had been at a conference in Vienna and had made this short side trip to the floating city to ride in a gondola and walk the streets together for a few days before heading home. After thirty years, they were still very much in love. They had invited me to dinner for the second night in a row, but I could tell, after we ate and strolled into the Piazza, that they wanted to be alone. Partly this was because they had come to this city to be together and I was making things decidedly less romantic, but it was also because I had gone on a rant at dinner about the dangerous promises of Luis Inácio Lula da Silva in their home country (this was in July, 2002 and the sweeping electoral victory of da Silva and his Workers' Party in Brazil had not yet happened). I had made a comparison between da Silva's socialist policy, which in my mind smacked of a politically dangerous naiveté, with government policy in Cambodia (a country which I'd been to just the month before), where Pol Pot had ordered genocide in the name of a "peasant agrarian society." The couple likely agreed with me. They no more supported da Silva then they did the thankfully long-defunct Khmer Rouge, but I had expressed myself somewhat too forcefully at dinner. Even if you happen to agree with the sentiment, it is the fashion of the post-modern intellectual elite not to trust such strong opinions, especially coming from someone you've just met. After the quintet had finished, I excused myself, the couple offered polite but distant goodbyes, and I went walking around by myself. The shadows were lengthening in the Piazza; I stood below the tall pedestal of the venerated statue of San Marco and watched the people crowding the bistros and strolling in the square. An old man was feeding pigeons; a juggler tossed burning wands into the air. The quintet started another piece — Bach this time — and suddenly I felt an underlying sense of importance and meaning: amid all this seemingly random accumulation of incident, amid the choices and decisions and pure accident that had brought me here, to this exact place, at this exact time, there lurked a sudden significance, an order, though what that significance was or meant I couldn't for the life of me fathom.

I have had this feeling before, a few times in my life. It comes on without warning, and it always happens when I am surrounded by people. The first time was at a high-school dance when I was sixteen. I was waltzing with a girl, I forget her name, and a song by the band Air Supply was playing on the speakers. I was struck by this same ineffable sense of pure meaning. It happened again ten years later in Ottawa. I was walking home from a friend's house one August night. There was a fire alarm ringing loudly in a building on one side of me, and a woman and a man screaming at each other in a parking lot on the other side. It was then that I felt it strongest — this idea that under all the randomness was a pattern and an order, almost an orchestration, and that in fact nothing was truly random.

Some people who have experienced such a thing have chalked it up to God, and have either become religious because of it or have had their faith verified. Not me. I choose to believe that these events mark some dramatic shift in my life and the way I perceive my life, some new epoch in my existence. In high school it was the passage from childhood to adulthood; in Ottawa, the passage from a painful, drug-laden existence to a new level of self-awareness. In Venice, too, I can put my finger on what change this sudden sense of meaning heralded.

The next day I was flying to Barcelona to meet my boyfriend, David. I had been travelling around Asia alone for the previous four months and I was looking forward to spending five weeks in Europe with him, to sharing the rest of my trip with him. If the Brazilian couple had taught me anything (besides keeping my politically volatile opinions to myself in the company of relative strangers), it was that the world in all its protracted variance is more gratifying when shared with someone you love. All my political passion about da Silva could not in any way match the passion those two elderly people felt for each other; and in the end, perhaps, that is why they felt so uncomfortable around me. For no matter how well-intentioned my ideas (and da Silva's and Pol Pot's), a political passion is ultimately a destructive one, while the passion that two people feel for each other is quite the opposite.

I went back to my hotel and started packing, and the next day I caught my nine o'clock flight to Frankfurt, for my connection to Barcelona where my lover was waiting.

II

98 | If this were a novel (but I hope not one of my own), this story would end here, and David and I would live happily ever after. This didn't happen. The five weeks of our trip was a kind of emotional hell. We fought everywhere. On the Eiffel Tower, atop the Arc de Triomphe, in the Musée D'Orsay, at the Forum in Rome, the bell tower in Pisa, the Prado in Madrid, on the cobbled streets of San Sebastian. We had good times, too. Travelling in Europe with David was like taking a course in musicology. In every city and town we visited, he knew the name of some obscure composer who had lived there, or had some interesting anecdote about those musicians everyone knew about. For one whole afternoon on the road from Paris to Amsterdam we listened to Shostakovich, and David held forth about the man's life, the death of his son, his trouble with Stalin, the creation of his masterpiece — *Lady Macbeth of Minsk.*

In Paris, we read *Giovanni's Room* aloud to each other in our small, inexpensive *pension* in the rue d'Austerlitz near the Gare de Lyons. We spent an entire day at the Louvre, determined to see it all, and somehow managed it, going from the Greek and Roman antiquities to those from Abyssinia and the Hittites in one breath. We made fun of the American crowds fighting for glimpses of the Mona Lisa, while other, more masterfully executed canvases by da

Vinci and Caravaggio hung ignored on the walls all around her. We irreverently photographed the Venus de Milo from behind, imagined riding naked on the *Winged Victory of the Samothrace*, stood in silent awe in front of Jean François David's *The Intervention of The Sabine Women*. (David noticed that the painter was fond of painting the perfect bare ass of one particular model over and over again in his pictures; we assumed this to be the artist's young *objet d'amour*.) We poked around the crypts at Père Lachaise cemetery and paid tribute at Oscar Wilde's grave.

And yet, despite all this, we still ended up screaming at each other in the middle of the night in the alley next to our hotel, saying things from which our relationship would never recover. When we came home three weeks later, David returned to Winnipeg and I to Ottawa. The relationship was over.

What wasn't over, however, was that sense I'd picked up in Italy that there had been some sea-change within me. I'd always been resigned to the probability that I would end up spending the rest of my life alone, or at least outside a sexually and (or) emotionally intimate relationship, like so many gay men I know. A friend of mine in Ottawa believes that gay men are not, for whatever reason, cut out to have long-term relationships. He believes that we should find the emotional intimacy and support we need from close personal friendships and family, and get our sexual intimacy from casual encounters with strangers, like a side order at a restaurant. I've tried this. And while it's true that I do have a number of close friends I can share practically anything with, a lover has always been a person I can share *everything* with. That to me is the essential difference, and primary importance, of a love relationship. Your friends get only pieces of you; your lover gets you entirely.

| 99

Another reason that I had decided it was tolerable to be alone for the rest of my life, prior to the Venice experience, was that I was a writer. A writer acquaintance told me once that her lovers always complained they always came second and the writing first. That has been my experience too. There have been times I wished I could have a lover to go to bed with who would disappear in the morning so I could get up and go the computer without all the attendant trouble of getting him breakfast. I write better in the morning. I find that if I get up and go right to work in my underwear, clutching only a cup of coffee and a cigarette, my internal editor doesn't have time to wake up, and I don't waste hours wondering if what I am writing is any good. I just write. Also, the state of mind required to write fiction has always been very similar in my experience to the dream state. And so, early in the morning, I sort of sleepwalk from my bed to my computer and continue dreaming, only this time with my fingers on the keyboard.

Having a boyfriend, and having to talk to him in the morning, always broke this spell. Even after just a few words of *Hello* and *How are you* and *What are we going to have for breakfast?* I found it harder to write, harder to bridge that gap between the real world and the fictional one I was trying to crawl into. When I was dating, I tried things like writing at night (which doesn't work as well for me) or writing after naps in the afternoon, and finally I tried refusing to have anyone stay over at all when I was working. This is all fine and well for someone you're dating casually, but for anyone serious, who wants to spend the rest of his life with you, it isn't going to work. I was better off alone, then. It was okay, wasn't it; because I was a writer and writers were supposed to be alone, weren't they?

Except for that thing that happened to me in Venice.

After David and I broke up and I returned to Ottawa, I found myself more restless than I had been before I travelled around the world. Whatever I had been looking for on that journey, it seemed I hadn't fully found it. I wasn't writing well then. My first novel was out, and I was waiting for my second to be published. I wanted to write a third, and I had a few ideas, but every time I sat down to write, all that came out was mush. And the restlessness was still with me. Gnawing at me daily, telling me that I had to *do* something without telling me exactly what. In January of 2003, I tried to quell it by getting a dog. As usual, I didn't think it through. One day I just started checking the Ottawa newsgroups for people who were giving away pets. I made trips to the Humane Society to scan the bulletin board for a suitable animal. I talked to a good friend of mine, a vet, about what kind of breed would suit me.

"A hound," he said. "Laid back, doesn't need a lot of exercise, good with cats and kids and very loyal."

"Do they shed?"

"Horribly."

"I don't want a dog who sheds."

"You can't have everything, Darren. No breed is perfect."

Good advice. (It also holds true for boyfriends.) That night I checked the webpage of the Humane Society; they had just posted a photograph of a new dog to be put up for adoption the following day. He was a three-year-old hound dog named Nixon. The next day at twelve when the adoption centre opened I went in to see him. When the staff member brought him out to meet me, his tail was down and he was trembling. He wouldn't look at me, but he didn't shy away from me either.

"He's been abused," said the trainer. "He's insecure and frightened most of the time, but he's gentle."

Good enough for me. I left him at the pound that night while I got the apartment ready, and the next day I brought him home. Little did I know at the time that this was a step in the right direction. I had owned cats for years, and as much as I loved them, I soon learned they don't require the same level of love and commitment that a dog does. I also realized that Nixon was going to screw up my writing routine entirely. He could not wait for me to get up, make coffee, and write for a couple of hours before I took him outside. The first morning I tried this he paid me back by promptly pissing and shitting on the kitchen floor.

So my dream state went out the window while I took him for his morning walk, when I would most likely meet a few other dog owners and be forced into conversation before I could get back to my keyboard. I've learned to write around Nixon's schedule, for, as much as he loves me, he couldn't care less about the new book I'm working on. He wants to play and to sniff in the morning, to lift his leg and spray all over the trunk of the nearest tree.

During the six months I had Nixon in Ottawa, I watched how my love nourished him. He began to sleep with me nights, instead of lying before the door whining to get out. His tail gradually lifted, and he stopped trembling and shying away from every quick movement and loud noise. A few problems remained. Lightning storms threw him into a terror for days. He threw up all over the interior of my new car every time I put him in it, and eventually I had to get plastic seat covers if I was to take him anywhere. (To this day he still gets terribly carsick.) I can't let him off the leash in the city, for he tends to follow his nose and doesn't always come back when called. He has no road sense whatsoever. Several times now he has run out into a busy street; I have to keep him on a very short leash when he's near traffic. But all in all, he is a much happier, healthier, more confident dog than he was when I first got him.

Nixon was my first great test in caring for and fully loving another creature. Ready for new challenges, and with a sense that I had not fulfilled the destiny that had been laid out for me in Venice, I made the decision to move from Ottawa to Toronto. I had always wanted to live in Toronto. When I was a boy in Nova Scotia, lying in my small, airless upstairs bedroom with the sloped ceilings and dreaming of one day being a writer, it was Toronto I always saw myself in. Never once did I picture myself in Ottawa, which to us in Nova Scotia was a land of politics and politicians and not much else. But when a friend of mine from university suggested I come up there and look for work, Ottawa is where I ended up, and where I stayed for eight years. While I was there, friend after friend left Ottawa for Toronto, and I hankered to do the same thing after each one moved away. Then, one Saturday, I found myself in the car driving down to the city to look at an apartment I had made an appointment to see just that morning.

I did not do this with a particular plan. At the time, it felt like the right thing to do, and I have always been a person who follows these kinds of instincts and have usually benefited from them. Less than a month later, I was living on Jarvis Street in the gay ghetto with my cats and Nixon.

The cats took some time adjusting, but Nixon liked it immediately. There were more dogs in Allen Gardens, the park around the corner from my building, and Toronto is a much more dog-friendly city than Ottawa. I liked it too. The new book was out. I was meeting people, doing interviews, trying new restaurants, and going to jazz concerts.

And dating.

Before I left Ottawa I had been lurking about a Toronto Internet chat room, trying to make new friends and maybe set up a few sexual contacts. I met this guy named Brian, who was from Mumbai and who had been in the French merchant-marine for nine years before moving to Toronto. We chatted for hours the first night we met online, and Brian seemed to think there was something special between us right away. My opinion of the situation differed somewhat. He was nice, but so were some of the other guys I'd met online. I decided that Brian was acting a little too serious for someone who didn't know me except through the medium of the Internet, and when I got to Toronto I didn't call him for a week or so while I played the field. Then, one night, I met him again on gay.com, and I thought *What the hell.* I asked him to come over.

Turned out, Brian lived right around the corner from me. The very first night we spent together he told me he wanted me to fall in love with him. My first thought was Glenn Close from *Fatal Attraction*, and I didn't call him for another two weeks. We spent a month or so emotionally wrestling with each other. Brian said he felt we were destined to be lovers. I wasn't so sure. Nixon, however, seemed to know something I didn't. They immediately fell in love with each other. When I went away, Brian took him in, and the two formed an even closer bond. I admit, I got a little jealous and I acted badly. I was determined to keep Brian at bay and continue seeing who I wanted. The exact moment when I gave in to him is not clear to me. But give in I did, though I was, as Brian has put it, "a lot of work." We have been together ever since. That feeling of restlessness I first began to feel with my revelation in Venice has left me, and another great epoch in my life has ended.

Or begun.

LESSON IN
CAMBODIA

                  I first heard about Cambodia in Thailand, while waiting for a passenger boat to the island resort of Ko Lanta. The boat was three hours late, and all the passengers, mostly young backpackers, were lounging on the grass next to the dock waiting for it to arrive. In Toronto, if a boat was three hours late, we'd all have been screaming at the ticket agents. But in Thailand, when a boat is late, you relax — you find a place to get out of the sun and sleep or read. (If only the West could adopt the Thai way of doing things, or if all of us could carry the attitude home.) We made lazy conversation, which turned, as it always does, to the places we'd been, the things we'd seen. A young British couple mentioned Cambodia.

"I've been there," said someone else. "Best part of my trip so far."

"Did you see the temples? Wasn't that incredible?"

"Did you go to the Cheung Ek? Siem Reap? Angkor Wat?"

The conversation turned again, to Laos and Vietnam. But I was intrigued by Cambodia. The name has always been on the edge of my memory — in some ways, uncomfortably so — ever since my father made me watch *The Killing Fields* with him when I was fifteen. I'd never considered going there when planning my itinerary in Southeast Asia. It never seemed to me, unlike Vietnam, Thailand, and Malaysia, a place you could actually go to. The next week, in Bangkok, I booked a flight to Phnom Penh.

* * *

Of course, not all the stories I heard about Cambodia were perfect. My guidebook to Southeast Asia recommended caution, especially when travelling on the national highways — highways that were so badly maintained it took forever to get anywhere and were prone to violent holdups: old fashioned, but no less dangerous for that, highway robberies. The book *Off the Rails in Phnom Penh: Into the Dark Heart of Guns, Girls, and Ganja* by Amit Gilboa chronicles the Phnom Penh of Western reputation — a violent, semi-lawless anarchy that has never entirely recovered from the atrocities of Pol Pot and the Khmer Rouge. I was nervous flying in. In China and Thailand I knew what to expect. In Cambodia, I didn't.

To my surprise, Phnom Penh was less hectic than I'd expected — a charming, French colonial city, with broader, less-crowded streets than Hanoi and green-shaded parkland running all along the Tonlé Sap River. There was the usual chaotic jumble of markets common in Asia, and vendors in the streets up from the river — selling everything from plastic combs and straw baskets and pirated DVDs to the ubiquitous spiny mounds of durian fruit. At night, the market outside my hotel reeked of rotted vegetables and urine, and packs of small children and dogs roamed the streets in equal number, looking for their next meal. Like most former colonial cities, Phnom Penh is an appalling mixture of poverty and wealth, with all the prejudices, reverse prejudices, and contradictions that that brings. The restaurants along the river cater to tourists and expatriates, with beer, hamburgers, and french fries going for about $7 American, but a local can get a plate of rice, fried beef, and a cup of tea in the market for twenty-five cents. I tried to get my hair cut on my second day there, and was turned away by three separate barbers, who refused to cut a foreigner's hair. Finally, one took me and gave me the best haircut of my life for a | 109 dollar.

For three days, I wandered about the city. I visited the National Museum — a hodgepodge collection of Buddhist and Brahman stone sculpture and images. Unlike in most museums I'd been to, the placement of the artifacts was haphazard. Ancient stone heads of Buddha sat on a card table; bronze casts of the many-armed Shiva stood on the floor in the corner; an ancient, twenty-foot-long bas-relief of Yama judging the sinners leaned precariously against one wall. You could touch them all. Nothing was alarmed; the floors were dirty and the rooms stuffy; there was no air-conditioning. It was like walking through someone's attic — the attic of Cambodia's past, stuffed with treasures from six thousand years of religious and artistic history.

There was no mention of the recent history we're all so familiar with — of Pol Pot and the Khmer Rouge, and the murder of two million Cambodians in the name of political ideology and the perfect communist collective. Pol Pot was a lunatic visionary who wanted to see his country restructured into an agrarian, peasant society. No wonder. Such a society couldn't read, didn't criticize, didn't talk back. In a period of seven years beginning in 1970, one-third of the Cambodian population was murdered. Richard Nixon and Henry Kissinger's decision to bomb Cambodia, which they saw as a possible hideout for Vietnamese communists, started the ball rolling by weakening the already tenuous hold of the Cambodian monarchy and allowing the Khmer Rouge to move from its small holdings in the interior of the country into the capital and beyond. A few years later, the Khmer Rouge had turned into one of the most brutal regimes in the world, and was presiding over an auto-genocide of one-third of the country's population — nearly two million people.

To find the history of the Khmer Rouge, one simply has to hire a motorbike and a driver to take you twelve kilometres east of Phnom Penh to the killing fields, known as Cheung Ek to most Cambodians. At first glance the fields are unimpressive — broad, overgrown expanses of sun-burnt, dun-coloured plains studded with gnarled yucca trees. But a closer look at the fifty-foot glass stupa in the centre of the first field reveals interior shelves, visible through the glass, that are lined with hundreds of human skulls: a delayed kind of witness to the atrocities once perpetrated here.

The Cambodian tendency for not designing, not fiddling, is apparent even here. As you walk through the fields, you see a worn pit dug into the earth decades ago. A hand-lettered sign pounded unceremoniously into the ground beside the hole states: "Mass Grave. 342 bodies found." Looking closely at the sloped, grass-covered sides of the pit, you can see bits of human bone and clothing. A large metal urn beside a tree is crammed with human femurs. Another hand-lettered sign beside a large tree states that this is where the babies were executed, by swinging them by their feet and smashing their skulls against the trunk. Everything is left to bear witness. Only the skulls are taken, and placed reverently inside the glass stupa. A trip back into Phnom Penh and the prison of Tuol Sleng, where prisoners were kept, interrogated, and tortured by the Khmer Rouge before being sent to Cheung Ek. Sometimes their only offence would have been the wearing of eyeglasses, which denoted 'intellectual' to the discriminating Khmer Rouge.

I had had enough. The next day I left the city, and travelled down the river to Siem Reap and the temples of Angkor Wat, hoping to balance the legacy of the Khmer Rouge with the ancient grandeur of the Cambodian temples. So much of Cambodia's history, and perhaps so much of the world's, is a journey from the sublime to the horrific and back to the sublime again.

| 111

* * *

The only way to get around Cambodia is by boat. As my guidebook said, the national highways are unpaved and rutted, so poorly maintained that a hundred-kilometre trip can take anywhere from ten to twenty hours on a bus. Also, in the semi-lawless interior of Cambodia, violent highway robberies still happen, so the boat from Phnom Penh to Siem Reap, along the Tonlé Sap river, is a steal, double meaning intended, at $75 American return. The only choice you need to make is between travelling in the hold of the twenty-foot-long speed boat, crowded in with forty other passengers without life jackets, or staying on the prow of the boat under the hot Cambodian sun, where your chances of surviving a sinking are better, but the likelihood of getting serious sunstroke is much worse. Being claustrophobic, a good swimmer, and naturally dark-skinned, I found the choice an easy one. I stayed above in the sun for five hours, used buckets of sunblock, and carried a book and a knapsack full of bottled water and stalks of watery rambutan fruit.

In the rainy season the trip by boat to Siem Reap (which, literally translated, means Siam defeated) can be less than four hours. But in July, when I was there, the river was low and muddy, fetid and still. The heat of the boat, however, tempted me to risk the liver flukes and other parasites for a quick dip. We envied the water buffalo, which stood up to their necks in the cool, muddy water, and only surged forward up onto the banks when our boat passed too near. Tanned, half-naked children swam and fished in the river in front of their huts, and waved furiously as we passed. We waved back, self-conscious at how white, how well-fed, how privileged we must have looked, with our knapsacks and baseball caps and dark glasses and sunblock smeared prissily across our noses. In some places the river was desperately narrow, and on two occasions our speedboat recklessly passed the small flat-bottomed wooden boats of fishermen without slowing, missing them by only a few feet, throwing water into their vessels, and threatening to swamp them. They did not shout, or yell, as they might have done in a Hollywood movie. They hardly looked up from their work, only gripped the sides of their little boats until the worst of our wake had passed by them and they could resume casting their nets.

There are times on any trip when the myths of what is expected merge with the reality of what is actually found, and these times become the most memorable, the most intense, of your journey. This was one of those times for me, when I felt as if I really was away from home and in a foreign environment. I'd felt this before on my travels, and it was not an entirely comfortable feeling. I was aware of the poverty I was seeing, which was intensified by the sudden awareness of my own relative comfort. But what is most memorable is not always the most pleasant. I knew, sitting on the boat and floating down a river through a jungle landscape fifteen thousand kilometres from the place where I was born, that I would remember this trip for the rest of my life.

* * *

We came to rest beside a raft twenty-seven kilometres south of Siem Reap and the temples of Ankgor Wat. Because the lake and river were so low, we were taken from our speedboat in flat-bottomed dugouts to the "floating village," which, at that time of year, was misnamed: it was the dry season, and the huts stood on stilts, not over water but over the stinking mud flats of the river. A crowd of touts — the common backpacker term for the hucksters who try to sell goods and services to tourists — jockeyed for position on the dock as we got out of the dugouts, eager to offer to drive us by motorbike into town. My passage was already arranged by my Phnom Penh hotel, and, sure enough, a young man with a cardboard sign with my name spelled incorrectly across it was waiting for me at the dock. He drove me by motorbike through the impoverished villages to Siem Reap, and my air-conditioned, marble-floored hotel. I made arrangements for him to pick me up early the next morning, when, for $7 American a day, he would guide me around the temples.

My guide's name was Lima, and as I found out the next morning, when we started out for the temples, his English was not good. My understanding of "guide" in this instance was grossly inadequate. Lima would drive me to the temples he thought of interest, and I would explore them on my own. For $2 a day I could have rented my own motorbike and done it myself, but there are so many temples, over such a wide geographical area, that having Lima around to act as an archaeological editor of sorts was an advantage. After much gesturing, and the translation efforts of a few of Lima's friends who were hanging about the hotel and who spoke better English, I ended up satisfied by this arrangement.

The temples cost $20 American a day to visit, or $40 for three days. The money goes not to the Cambodian government but to the petroleum giant Sokimex, which arranged the deal years ago with the help of a few local politicians. There is a central gate along the paved road into the jungle and the temples where you buy your pass. The three-hundred-odd square kilometre jungle area housing the temples is not fenced. There's no need. Cambodia has the largest concentration of unexploded land mines of any country in the world. Straying off the beaten paths, even within fifteen metres of some of the temples, can be extremely dangerous, and picking your way into the temple area through the jungle to avoid the entrance fees just might end up costing you, literally, an arm and a leg.

For three days, I visited the glorious temples of Siem Reap and the ancient Khmer civilization. The Khmers (not to be mistaken with the Khmer Rouge) were at their societal and cultural peak between the ninth and eleventh centuries of the Christian era. Their religious practices were a mix of Brahmanism, brought from India, and worship of the local gods and goddesses, all of which transmuted itself in later years by some creative evolution to the Buddhism that has subsumed much of Southeast Asia. The architecture of Angkor Wat reflects this mix, with perfectly preserved bas-relief drawings and friezes depicting Brahman figures such as Shiva and Yama beside the Khmer Apsara dancers. (These depictions, which adorn the walls of the temples, are some of the most beautiful and well-preserved examples of relief carving in the world.) Amidst all this, in the ruins of the temples, Buddhist shrines have been placed, and the temples are crawling with monks in saffron robes, busily engaged in the daily business of their faith — lighting incense, meditating, begging for alms.

On the second day at the temples, Lima insisted I get up at dawn to see the sun rise above the three towers of the most famous temple in the region. Afterwards, and somewhat groggily, I explored the giant temple itself, named Angkor Wat, from which the region has taken its name. I spent an hour alone walking the length of the east outer gallery looking at a bas-relief of the Hindu creation myth, *The Churning of the Ocean of Milk*. It was here that I met a young saffron-robed monk named Yaya. He was wandering under the outer galleries to avoid the sun, and, as I found out later, playing hooky from a morning's work in his Buddhist temple a few hundred yards away in the jungle.

Arranging his robe about his legs, Yaya sat down with me on the stone floor of the outer gallery and proceeded to speak in his broken English. He was twenty-two, and had been living in the monastery since he was five. His parents had been murdered by the Khmer Rouge, and the local monks had stolen the toddler away and hidden him in the attic of the monastery. He stayed there, unbeknownst to the authorities, for three years, being fed and cared for by the monks. When the Vietnamese officially defeated the Rouge in 1977, young Yaya was offered permanent sanctuary in the monastery, with the understanding that he would one day take vows and become a monk, to repay in spiritual currency the monks who had saved him. He had done so, and has been there ever since.

It was a sad, beautiful story, with one hitch: Yaya didn't want to be a monk anymore.

"I want to be a tour guide and save enough money to move to America," he told me, smiling, and destroying forever my Hollywood ending. He left shortly after to go back to work at the monastery, but not before he borrowed some money from me for cigarettes and chocolate.

116 With Yaya's story still fresh in my mind, I climbed up to the topmost gallery of the temple, and sat on the highest parapet overlooking the jungle. I had come to Cambodia, to Asia, seeking something. In the back of my mind was the vague notion that I would become a Buddhist, and perhaps I was looking for a revelation, a transformation, the thing that so many Western men and women are looking for when they travel to far-off destinations and so rarely ever find.

What I found in Cambodia after talking with Yaya *was* a revelation of sorts, and a spiritual one at that, though I could never have predicted its nature. It was the same revelation I had when I first went to Paris looking for the literary romance of Montparnasse, the home of expatriates like Hemingway and Fitzgerald. The music, adventure, and romance that I thought were playing out in other lives and in other cultures and other locations were either not playing there or were indistinguishable from the music playing in my own.

Not that there was no magic in the world, but the magic existed in *all* the world, my world as well, in equal proportion with the rote, the usual, and the familiar.

It was a great irony: here was Yaya seeking his dream — secular pleasure and security and living in America — and here I was, loaded down with what *he* was seeking, and I unable anymore to appreciate it, looking instead for what he had: a quiet life of contemplation and enlightenment.

That day I realized it is desire itself that keeps us moving, that keeps us seeking, that keeps us running. The desire for love, for money, for power. Even for spiritual enlightenment and everlasting life.

Desire is the reason I had come to Cambodia. |117

Desire is the reason Yaya wanted to leave it.

Desire is the reason that Pol Pot committed all those crimes against his own people.

Desire is the reason that the twin towers came down, and the world reacted so insanely afterwards.

Desire, not situation, is the thing, or so say the Buddhists, that causes us all our misery. And so there I sat — high above the Cambodian jungle on the parapet of an ancient temple built by a race that had long since disappeared and taken its secrets with it — finally understanding this first and most ancient lesson.

CALLING
AGAMEMNON

I love Hollywood movies. The bigger — the cheesier — the better. When it comes to books, I want quality. I want politics, innovation, social relevance, fantastic description, and a brilliant story to boot. One of my favourite books is Dostoevsky's *The Brothers Karamazov* because it provides all these things in one, albeit exceptionally hefty, package.

But I don't expect nearly as much from the film industry. All I really want from a movie is to be entertained. That's not to say there aren't thoughtful, important, culturally savvy films being made. There are, though Hollywood does not often engage in this kind of endeavour. Film is an art like any other medium, and there are some profound things happening on celluloid these days. But when I go out to a film on a Friday or a Saturday night, I rarely go to my local art-house cinema around the corner where these types of films (some good, some bad, some simply pretentious) are being shown on a regular basis. Rather, I head to the nearest multi-screened extravaganza, with the smell of overpriced, artery-clogging popcorn and Hollywood cheese in the air. I want to sit in front of a screen and eat popcorn and drink soda and simply not think for an hour or two. I want to be utterly swept away in a world of fantasy or romance or hilarity or suspense.

I read once that the philosopher Ludwig Wittgenstein did the same thing. He would select a few students from his college at Cambridge to accompany him to the cinema in the afternoon, where he would sit in the exact centre of the theatre so that the giant white screen filled his entire field of vision, and he would not be forced to think about anything but the scenes flashing in front of him. And although I make no claims to have the kind of mind Wittgenstein had, I certainly can relate. Perhaps it is because I'm a writer. I love to write stories. I live to write them. But stories are not all entertainment and fun. I try to ask (though rarely achieve) the same standards of the stories that I write as I do of the stories I read — that they be both entertaining and meaningful. By the end of the week, after struggling with the craft and art and the demands of writing (even if those demands are self-imposed), I want something light, something fun, something meaningless and mindless to take my mind off the day's literary struggles.

I don't want *Kandahar* or *The Apple* (both excellent films of the meaningful variety). I want *Pretty Woman*. I want *Field of Dreams*. I want *The Lord of the Rings*. That doesn't mean that I'll put up with just anything. I don't want *Twister* or *Battlefield Earth* — something that sets out simply to entertain and fails miserably at that. As any writer knows, entertaining for the sheer fun of it is hard work, and takes nearly as much talent as writing something with meaning. The best films are those that entertain you so well you don't even notice you're being profoundly instructed at the same time. But those films are rare, and so difficult to achieve that only one or two may come along in a decade. So, given the lack of both entertaining and culturally instructive films, I am not ashamed to admit, once more, that I enjoy Hollywood crap.

II

My latest foray into the world of crapola is the Hollywood block- | 121
buster *Troy*, starring the blonde-haired hunk Brad Pitt. I have to
admit, even I had misgivings about Hollywood's intrusion into the
world of Homer and *The Iliad*. I first read *The Iliad* in Turkey in a
small hotel not far from the ruins of Troy, where the three-thou-
sand-year-old story supposedly took place. It was one of the great
reading experiences of my life. I still remember how moved I was
when Homer describes the final showdown between Achilles and
Hector, as the former chases the latter round and round the outer
walls of Troy, and, as Homer puts it, all the gods stop to watch. In
all of Greek mythology (and perhaps literature as a whole), I don't
believe this moment has its equal. When did *all* the gods — self-
involved, morally impoverished creatures that they are, like the
men who created them — ever stop together to silently watch an
event in the affairs of men, except for this one? Thus was Homer's
genius — to say so much in a single line that would so resonate
down the ages to my hotel room in Turkey, some ten thousand
miles from home, and move me to sympathetic tears.

As entertained and instructed as I was by the epic poem, I was
not quite sure that I approved of my favourite pop-culture franchise
turning the ambrosia of Homer into intellectual hamburgers and

french fries. But of course I went. I had to go, if only to see what a muck they would make of it. And according to the critics, or most of them anyway, make a muck of it they did.

Many were offended by the fact that they changed the story so much. (I can easily picture the boorish Samuel Goldwyn in a storyboard meeting for the film saying, "Who is this shmuck, Homer, anyway, and how much are we paying him?") The film covers the entire Trojan war, not just the fifty-five day interlude of *The Iliad*. Worse, it seems to intimate that the war lasted about a week, instead of the ten years that Homer says it took. It plays up the enmity between Agamemnon and Achilles. It makes brothers Agamemnon and Menelaus unrepentant villains, which is a small violation not only of the plot but of the spirit of the poem. It ignores the gods entirely, as well as other heroes such as Aeneas and Ais and Diomodes. Patroclus becomes Achilles' cousin (instead of his lover, as most Homeric interpreters agree he was). There are a whole host of violations—some for technical reasons, some for dramatic reasons, some for none other than the perverse pleasure Hollywood screenwriters (and producers, as the case may be) take in changing a story from the way it was originally written.

The most damaging reviews of the movie came from the group of teenagers I overheard standing outside the theatre after it was over. "That sucks," said one. "I almost fell asleep," said another. "What a waste of thirteen bucks," lamented a third.

This was the everyman version of the critic's estimation that the film "lacked heart" and failed to "engage" the audience. Imagine my own surprise when, despite all the inaccuracies and heavy-handedness in the screenplay, I found myself wanting to defend the film. It's true that Brad Pitt couldn't act his way out of a paper bag (though he looked damned fine throughout, even when he was covered in Trojan blood and gore. That man can wear anything and get away with it!) There was something about the film that attracted me despite all its obvious flaws. Upon thinking about it, I realized in its portrayal of the Trojan war, the movie was essentially Homeric.

What I mean by that statement is this: when I read Homer my first thought was that the Greeks and the Trojans, and the civilization that produced them, were savage, as Tennyson put it. All that blood and violence! The scene where a fallen Trojan soldier begs red-haired Menelaus on his knees for his life, and the latter, at his brother's urging, kills him anyway! Homer, upon first glance, seems to approve of all this slaughter. He calls all his characters — Trojan and otherwise — "great" and "noble" and "redoubtable," and invents countless other honorifics for them. One minute he is describing in heroic terms the death of a group of Trojans at the hands of the Greeks, and a few pages later, he is describing with equal enthusiasm the murder of a band of Greeks at the hands of the bloodthirsty Trojans. He seems to take great delight in all the gory details, telling over and over again of spears penetrating the backs of necks, of swords slicing off tongues at the base, tearing through bronze, and hewing into flesh. He spends much time on the beauty of the warriors' armour and much less on the ugliness of their killer dispositions.

Because of this, The Iliad, beautifully written as it is, is almost a base pleasure at first, like watching a Claude Van Damme flick. At some points you find yourself rooting for the Achaeans (Greeks) when one of their number is savagely killed by the Trojans. Then, when the revenge attack is so brutal that you lose sympathy for the revenger, you go over to the side of Trojans. Then the Trojans counter-revenge and you lose sympathy for them, and flee back to the Achaeans. Carried along by the glorious description and caught up in the violence, you almost feel as if you are on the battlefield with both armies, engaging in this bloodiest of wars.

And then, a strange literary alchemy begins to take place. You slowly start to disentangle yourself from the war altogether, to withdraw intellectually from the fighting, just as Achilles did, to sit by himself in the Greek camp and refuse to partake. But for the reader the reasons for this withdrawal are nobler than those of Achilles. The endless cycle of revenge and counter-revenge begins to seem hopelessly futile, pointless. In the place of rooting for one side or the other, you feel a feel a kind of helpless, overwhelming pity for everyone involved, which culminates in the dreadful pathos of Achilles chasing poor Hector around the walls of Troy and the anguished wailing of Andromache, Hector's wife, when her husband finally is killed by Achilles.

Here the glory of war collapses, and you are left with only sorrow. It is no coincidence that Homer's poem ends with the Trojan king, Priam, sneaking into the Achaean camp to ask for his son's body back from the ruthless Achilles, which he succeeds in obtaining. Thus, the only fruitful encounter between the two armies, or representatives thereof, takes place, according to Homer, not through violence but through appeals to compassion and humanity.

Through negotiation.

There Homer's book fittingly ends. Given what is going on in the world today — Iraq, Palestine, Israel, Afghanistan, North Korea, the Congo, the Sudan, Tibet — this is a lesson, three thousand years in the making, and that no one seems to want to learn. Of course, the movie in some way misses the point. By following the Trojan war to its bloody conclusion – – the sack of Troy (the Hollywood folks couldn't resist showing the Trojan Horse being pulled through the city gates) — Homer's moral is blunted. It's unlikely that many North American moviegoers have read the poem in translation, and very few of us will actually see any real war beyond what is portrayed in front of us on the big and little screens, so the movie will do. What *Troy* does in its limited, Hollywood-chic way is refuse to present us with any heroes, which is true to the spirit of Homer. The violence and action goes back and forth, back and forth, just as Homer described it (thought not nearly as eloquently or as beautifully). And that is why those teenagers standing outside the cinema didn't like the film: it gave them no hero to root for.

We have created a generation, perhaps a succession of them, that believes one side always has to be right and the other side wrong. That is the reason why we are neck-deep in the quagmire of Iraq, and embroiled in all those other places I mentioned. If our combined history since the Trojan war has proved anything, it is that no one side is ever entirely right, or wrong. War is simply a clash of world views, and tragedy always results, no matter how good our intentions. I'm no fan of Saddam Hussein. But neither am I a fan of our own leaders. Most of us are so caught up in the hateful blood-rush of revenge and counter-revenge that we have refused to see the truth of what Homer taught us nearly three thousand years ago — that war never accomplishes what it sets out to do.

Even a supposed victory doesn't guarantee us anything. The story of the Trojan war did not end with the fall of Troy. There is

Homer's *The Odyssey*, and Virgil continues the story in *The Aeneid* several hundred years later. When the Trojan Aeneas escapes Troy after its fall, he founds Rome, which eventually goes on to capture and enthrall Greece, the legendary winners of the first war. Thus the cycle of revenge and counter-revenge continues, and plays out long after the walls of Troy have fallen.

I only wish those teenagers — not much younger, I would guess, than some of those fighting right now in the Middle East — could see and understand what Homer and Virgil were trying to say. I only wish that those blind Agamemnons at the head of our nations could see and understand that if we persist in waging war, no matter what happens tomorrow in Iraq and no matter what the reasons we give for going or staying there, one day our walls too will fall.

MARCEL DUCHAMP,
A NEW AESTHETIC AND
BUZZ ALDREN'S MOON

I first encountered the art of Marcel Duchamp in the Tate Modern Gallery in London in the summer of 2000. This was, in fact, the first summer that this now-famous gallery was opened on the south bank of the Thames, in a converted power station. The massive open space at the front of the gallery which used to house the giant turbines that supplied the vast English capital with its electricity, was now dominated by cafés and gift shops and a permanent exhibit of great black iron-sculpted spiders by New York artist Louise Bourgeois. I had gone to the gallery that day with my friend, the American novelist Eric Shaw Quinn, who was living in London at the time. Both of us were long past the giggle and my-two-year-old-nephew-could-do-better stage of viewing contemporary art, and so we went to the new gallery with the serious intention of enjoying and discussing the painting, sculpture, and other works installed there.

By and large, it was a relaxing afternoon. Eric and I enjoyed and understood most of what we saw, and if we didn't understand it, we could at least fathom, after some initial discussion, the reasoning behind it. At one point, I was passing through a construction area that had a worktable littered with tools and sawdust and an empty yogurt cup, and I was thinking that the room should have been blocked off, only to realize that we were smack dab in the centre of an exhibit. It was a "deliberately constructed" construction, a way of making us look twice at rooms like this through which we pass all the time. I remember taking another look, at the way the yogurt cup, turned on its side with pink fluid still drying inside, took on a new resonance, a new meaning. Someone had deliberately, carefully, placed that cup there, and was now asking me to look at it in ways I never had done before.

That, to me, is what a lot of modern art is about. Taking a second look. Here the banal is elevated to the artistic by the will of the artist so that the viewer can reconsider its relationship to himself, and his relationship to it. I understood that perfectly then, and still do today. One of the artists responsible for this change in the way we think about art, and how that art relates to the viewer, was represented in the gallery that day, and Eric and I ended up having one of our longest, and most heated discussions about him. I am talking of the French artist Marcel Duchamp, who some say has had more influence than any other artist on the art of the twentieth century.

* * *

We often hear contemporary and modern art referred to as conceptual art, art that requires understanding on an intellectual or conceptual level, which is different from representational art, art that makes immediate visual sense and stimulates some kind of sensual recognition. This idea that modern art must be related to a concept is why, I suppose, so many modern artists give us a written explanation of their work, why manifestos have become almost obligatory for all new camps of artistic endeavour since the Dadaists took intellectual Paris by storm after the First World War. It is true that much of what we call modern art, rather than relying on a purely visual recognition of the subject matter, requires an intellectual understanding of what the artist is attempting to do. But the matter, I would argue, is not always conceptual or intellectual. Meret Oppenheim's *Fur-lined Cup, Saucer, and Spoon,* | 129 for example, is a work of surrealist art that appeals not to our mind but to our visceral senses. The idea of drinking out of a teacup lined with fur on the inside causes, in me at least, a palpable revulsion, and, ultimately, it is through this very physical reaction that I re-evaluate my position to fur and cups and these otherwise normal objects. (The surrealists, more than most artists in the twentieth century, relied on an instinctive, emotive, non-conceptual, intuitive approach to art.) The art of Picasso and Matisse, of Jasper Johns and Mark Rothko, as obtuse or over-simplified as all these artists can sometimes be, often render subjects that elicit first an emotive and *then* an intellectual response (such as sex, patriotism, violence, religion, spirituality, etc.), which is what artists since the time of the ancient Greek sculptor Praxiteles have been asking us to do.

What makes modern art different from what went before, in my opinion, is not concept per se, but con*text.* When an Impressionist master painted a bowl of fruit or a sunrise, most contemporary audiences have the context to be able to understand what the artist is getting at. We have seen a bowl of fruit and a sunrise before, and so can judge both an artist's intention in painting it in the first place and how well it has been executed.

The same cannot be said for Picasso's *Guernica*, or Rochenberg's white canvases. The context for these works is largely intellectual, historical, and subjectively emotive. To understand and appreciate them fully, you must understand not just the historical subject but also the history of art and painting, the developments in art prior to the time they were created, the popular reaction to them, and against them, and the artist's personal oeuvre and attempts to create an art based on non-visual or non-aesthetic principles. Artists sometimes provide an explanation of their art to help you along with this (where the idea came from, what its antecedents were, what were his or her intentions in creating the piece), but, even with this coaching, modern art asks so much more of its audience than did most of the art of previous centuries. And that is why so many people have been left behind.

130 |

Most people do not have the time, the inclination, or the energy, to educate themselves. Who has time to study art history and read a biography of the artist in order to understand where Andy Warhol fits into the scheme of things? Who has time to read all the old myths and T.S. Eliot in order to understand the work of Robert Motherwell that is now hanging at the Art Gallery of Ontario in Toronto? If you had never read *The Divine Comedy*, you could still appreciate Rossetti's panels of Beatrice and Dante because they at least *look* like real people. In effect, modern artists ask the viewer to do half the work, to participate in art in an unprecedented way. There was, and is, no longer any silver platter. Without the prerequisites for understanding, without the proper *context*, most modern art has become increasingly difficult, recondite, abstruse, and remote. Much of it appeals only to other artists and a few select patrons, and the halls of modern art galleries will always abound with puzzled stares, giggles, snorts of laughter, and sighs of disgust. Tomorrow's newspapers will always carry a scandal or two about how many tax dollars were paid for this red stripe on that blue background, or what is considered pornography and not art. A number of viewers, without the necessary context to evaluate, will pretend to get what they see anyway, and it is this lack of knowledge, this lack of context, that opens up the doors to frauds and charlatans to display their work alongside those who do know what they're doing, and who have made a careful study of the art of the century so that theirs can contribute and move it forward.

Some consider this a sad state of affairs indeed (though I don't), and one of the artists most often blamed for this "breakdown in communication" between art and society is Marcel Duchamp.

* * *

Before that day at the Tate Modern in July of 2000, I, like many of the non-gallery going people I have met in my lifetime, had never heard of Marcel Duchamp. Neither had my friend Eric, but both of us were intrigued when we came across his *Fountain* installed under a glass case in the centre of one of the rooms.

Fountain is a urinal. Duchamp did not sculpt it, as I first thought, but bought it from a foundry and entered it as a sculpture in the "open" exhibition of the Society of Independent Artists in New York City (where it was never displayed) and signed it R. Mutt, 1917. The version that we saw at the Tate was not the original (which was lost, or deliberately smashed, depending on which version of the story you read), but was one of four reproductions made under the exacting eye of the artist a few years before his death in 1968. Out of all of the exhibits that afternoon, this was the one that made Eric and me stop and ask the age-old question: "What is art exactly?"

The *Fountain* is now famous because it has been provoking that very question more or less ever since it was first "created." (Duchamp insisted that choosing an object to be called art was itself an act of creation, whether that object was made in a foundry or on a sculptor's pottery wheel or was a cast-off yogurt cup.) I am both proud and ashamed to admit that, on the one hand, I immediately understood what Duchamp was trying to do with his sculpture (or "ready-made," as he liked to call these pieces), and on the other, I dismissed it as non-art.

Eric wasn't so sure. He thought the *Fountain* could technically be called art because the artist intended it to be so.

"What is the purpose of art?" I asked him. "I thought it was a matter of communication, and not intention."

"It is for me," Eric answered. "As it is for you." (Both of us were writers of fiction, and communication, the work of Gertrude Stein aside, almost always needs to be the purpose of writing.) "But maybe it wasn't for Duchamp," Eric went on. "Maybe his purpose was to provoke. To make you think about urinals, about the *idea* of urinals, the way the construction room made you think about yogurt cups and worktables."

For two hours Eric and I sat outside the gallery under the ubiquitous and infamous London cloud cover and argued about art. The argument petered out when Eric, a former philosophy major, dragged Spinoza into it. (The ideas of Spinoza, like the idea of God, will always leave any well-intentioned discussion dead in the water.) By the end of our *Fountain* discussion, we had agreed on little. I still didn't think the *Fountain* was art, Eric did, and neither of us were doing such a great job of explaining why. I only came to understand later that it was the fracturing of the consensus about what art is and is not that characterizes the art philosophy and history of the twentieth century, and that the reason I came to see Duchamp as important is because it was largely his work that started this fracturing. Indeed, some believe this was the sole point of his work entirely, and that Duchamp, rather than Picasso or Matisse (who were largely visual artists working within a certain visual tradition, albeit expanding it radically), who stands as the intellectual and spiritual father of the art of the twentieth century. Because of this controversy, however, Marcel Duchamp has been called many things throughout the century — a charlatan, a fraud, a visionary, a genius, a prophet. Along with the urinal, he chose as ready-made sculpture a snow shovel (*In Advance of the Broken Arm*); a bicycle wheel; a bottle-drying rack; and a birdcage full of marble cubes, a thermometer and the bone of a cuttlefish (the enigmatically titled *Why Not Sneeze, Rose Selavy?*). He created a number of machines and mechanical devices that are often considered the world's first examples of the installation art that now dominates contemporary galleries. At one point, he even considered signing the Woolworth building in Manhattan and claiming it as the world's tallest piece of ready-made sculpture. (Something he never got around to doing, and which in my opinion makes the art world, and New York City, a poorer place for it.) He tried photography and filmmaking, writing, and even cross-dressing as a form of artistic expression. He broke every rule and convention of his time, and, by so doing, anticipated every single major artistic innovation in a century whose art, when all is said and done, may still be remembered more for its spirit of innovation and development than for the actual physical objects that resulted from it.

As the German composer Arnold Schönberg said of his American music student, the avant-garde composer John Cage, Duchamp was perhaps less an artist than "an inventor of genius." Picasso and Matisse are known as the most important stylistic artists of the century, whereas Duchamp sought to eliminate the benevolent tyranny of style from his work entirely, and perhaps it is fitting that, if you polled the average person on the street, most would never have heard of him.

* * *

When Buzz Aldren stepped off the Eagle moon unit after Neil Armstrong, he was moved to utter the words "magnificent desolation" in response to his first view of the gorgeous but sterile lunar landscape. Whenever I think of this phrase, I tend to think of it as an almost perfect description of the landscape of the art of the twentieth century, perhaps of the entire century itself. So much of what happened in that century is magnificent, simply because it was so risqué and violent and new, and so much of it is, at the same time, desolate, because it lacks all the sensory richness and mystique and traditional aesthetic appeal, what I heard one man describe once as the "aura," of what has gone before. And although I appreciate the meaning of this desolation, and I do not vilify artists like Duchamp who insist on bringing all the ugliness and mechanization of the world to our attention, I cannot help feeling that it is the call of artists of the next century to find a new aesthetic. I have no idea what this will look like. Much of the art I see in galleries today is interesting and occasionally compelling, but not new or unusually innovative. And some of what we celebrate as art is downright devoid of originality, is as sterile as the landscape of Aldren's moon. Salvador Dali once wrote: "The first man to compare the cheeks of a young woman to a rose was obviously a poet; the first to repeat it was possibly an idiot." Perhaps a new technology will pave the way for a new set of metaphors in art, just as photography is credited with spawning the revolution in the art of the twentieth century. Until then, it is the job of all artists, those of us who work with words as well as those who use paint and other media, to understand and incorporate the developments of the century into our work as best we can. For those who can do this, and at the same time, like Duchamp, find a new set of expressions to do it with, we reserve Schönberg's title, "Inventor Of Genius."

OSCAR WILDE
AND THE WINDS
OF CHANGE

I met Stephen on the first day of rehearsals for the Winds Of Change theatre troupe. Those of us lucky or talented enough to be cast (most fell firmly into one category or the other) showed up at the theatre promptly at eight on Saturday morning and were let in by John, the theatre manager.

The director arrived late. Some decades before she had spent a year living in Italy with her now ex-husband and had never managed to readjust to that peculiar North American custom of being on time. So we actors stood around in the decaying lobby of the Astor Theatre in the small, seaside town of Liverpool, Nova Scotia, smoking cigarettes and drinking coffee out of styrofoam cups from the diner next door. We speculated endlessly on who would get what part. Brenda, the director, didn't like to tell us what part we had when she called after auditions to tell us we were cast. She preferred, she said, to see our faces when she broke the wonderful news.

Wonderful news, all right — unless you tried out for Hamlet and ended up as Guard #1. I use this as an example only. The

Winds of Change never did Shakespeare. There were those in the upper echelons of the amateur troupe who believed none of us had the requisite language skills.

In my opinion, Brenda liked it just as much to see the crest-fallen, the downtrodden, when they found out they didn't get the part they wanted. I was confident I had secured one of the two male leads. Brenda liked me, and there were no other men of note waiting in the lobby to challenge me. Stephen — the blue-eyed, blonde, illustrious Stephen — had not yet arrived. Like Brenda, though he had never been to Italy, he was chronically late for everything. Later he told me he was *born* with European sensibilities.

The play to be performed that year was *The Importance Of Being Earnest*. This was a bit risqué for our little troupe and our little town. God knows if the coterie of grey-haired ladies and gentleman who frequented our performances would approve. It was 1987 and I was nineteen years old. Poor Oscar had been sentenced to hard labour ninety years before. He had served his time and promptly died thereafter in exile in France. But in Liverpool, which had retained certain of the Victorian sensibilities, there was no statute of limitations on perversion. There would be those among the audience who would be scanning the text for hints of unnatural carnality, and watching the actors with more than a casual interest.

Which is why there were few men in the theatre that day. Most Winds of Change productions brought out as many men as women. This time there were only three male actors — me, David and Vernon. Vernon was a middle-aged, overweight, balding school-teacher who was in most productions of the troupe. In the dramas, he played bit parts (he was to be, we all correctly surmised, the

Reverend Chasuble), but the fall musicals were where he really shone. He had a lovely high tenor voice, and like many big men, for some mysterious reason, he was a wonderful dancer. It was not a musical unless Vernon got to glide across the stage and bring the audience to its feet. No one, not even the most jealous of the other actors, resented him for it. Vernon was an impossibly nice guy — timid and sweet and genuine, with a soft-spoken effeminacy that made him perfect for the part of Reverend Chasuble.

David was a different story. Although he didn't know it, or wouldn't admit it to himself, he was destined to play Lane — footman to Algernon and the smallest role in *Earnest*. He always got a small role, though he was one of the most capable and versatile actors in the troupe. Except no one could stand him. Not cast, not crew, not the director; nor even a vast majority of the audience. To have David in a lead would be never to hear the end of it. And so, abilities aside, he would always be cast in a supporting role, where he would nurse his resentments and spend the three months of rehearsals thinking up the little touches he would need to add to his role to upstage and upset the others. Sometimes, if the play was classical, the director would cast David as the mustachioed villain — a role which suited him and the audience perfectly. But alas, Brenda didn't go in for villainous drama. So David would play the footman. By day he worked as a clerk at the Post Office, where he had no ambitions other than to be rude to the customers and uphold to the letter the maddening paper bureaucracy of the Post Office. Thus in real life he was a footman also of sorts.

As far as male roles went, that left me. There were two, of which I would get to play only one: Jack, the straightlaced suitor in love with Gwendolen and terrified of Aunt Augusta; or Algernon, the dandy. Algernon was the more challenging of the two roles, but also the riskiest. For as Oscar Wilde most certainly intended but never actually admitted, Algernon would have been considered gay by everyone who saw the play when it was first produced in London, and is considered so by everyone who has seen the play ever since, including the aforementioned coterie of old ladies and gentlemen, the self-appointed purveyors of what was tasteful and decorous and proper in all small towns from Liverpool, Nova Scotia to Shropshire, England and beyond.

Enter Stephen: blonde, soft-skinned, handsome, but anaemic; enveloped in a gentle, blue-eyed, adolescent cynicism and spiritual ennui from which he would never entirely recover and would never really want to. As he came sauntering into the lobby of the theatre, smoking a Gitane and drinking a fresh latte out of a styrofoam cup, I knew in a flash who was going to be who in our little amateur production.

Stephen would be Algernon and I would be Jack.

And thus it would remain, long after the final curtain had closed.

* * *

I'd first heard about Oscar Wilde from our high-school principal, who was forced, perhaps on pain of death, to substitute-teach one of our Grade eleven English classes one afternoon when our regular teacher got sick and had to go home. The arrangement was sudden, and the principal — who had majored in Phys. Ed. and looked and acted more like an RCMP officer than an educator — had no experience or knowledge of our current work of study, *Heart of Darkness*. He decided to lecture us on the one writer he did know something about — the Irish author Oscar Wilde.

Wilde, he told us, was, without a doubt, one of the worst repro-
bates in the history of literature.

He was gay.

He was effeminate.

He was witty, in a mean, clever but provincially catty way.

Like Socrates, he was a corrupter of youth.

Like Socrates, he had a trial. | 141

Like Socrates, he lost.

Unlike Socrates, who was forced to drink hemlock, Wilde was
locked away in Reading Gaol and sentenced to hard labour until
he was released in 1897, dying three years later in France from
overwork and a broken heart (a peculiarly Victorian malady).

Socrates last words were "Crito: I owe a cock to Asclepias. Will
you remember to pay the debt?" The supposed last words of Oscar
Wilde were "Either this wallpaper goes, or I do."

I have to admit, despite the homophobic vitriol of his account,
the principal did make Wilde's life entertaining to us sixteen-year-
olds (small wonder, as vitriol is the chief weapon in any teenager's
emotional arsenal). The chief effect of this story was to impress
upon me, and likely every other member of that class, the image
of Wilde as an untalented but entertaining pervert who eventually
got what was coming to him. It's amazing to me that a hundred
years later this image of Wilde still persists, and not just in under-
informed teenagers.

The novelist John Irving has said that Wilde will be remembered
chiefly for his conversation and not his writing. (This statement
was made a hundred years after Wilde's death, as if a century was
the normal run for the work of any artist.)

George Bernard Shaw said after Wilde's death that he couldn't believe that *The Importance of Being Earnest* represented the playwright's mature artistic achievement (though in later years Shaw did relent and say he learned his sense of wit from Wilde).

James Whistler maintained till the end of his days that Wilde was a talentless hack, but Whistler was a friend of Wilde's until he turned jealous rival, so his opinion perhaps can be discounted.

Wilde has had his admirers as well. Winston Churchill, when asked what famous historical figure of note he would like to engage in conversation with, didn't hesitate to put Wilde at the top of the list. Generations of writers, such as Max Beerbohm, H.L. Menken, Dorothy Parker, G.K. Chesterton, Noel Coward, and Somerset Maugham, have all acknowledged an indebtedness to him. To this day, Hollywood has retained a fascination with his life and his work. (The most recent film productions of his plays, two of them starring that superficial dandy of modern times, Rupert Everett, have been overproduced pieces of crap that I'm sure Wilde himself would have despised.) The English writer and actor Stephen Fry played Wilde in the critically acclaimed eponymous film, which was itself based on the hugely successful biography of Wilde by respected biographer Richard Ellman, who died of AIDS just a few years after completing it. And if this is not testament enough to Wilde's abilities as a writer, as well as thinker and maker of epigrams, his essay *De Profundus*, addressed to his young lover, Lord Alfred Douglas, and written while he was in prison, was sealed up in a vault for seventy years after his death because the information it contained was deemed too damaging to the individuals and the society it named.

Wilde had been paid the greatest compliment afforded to any writer of any age: that of censorship.

Like Socrates, Wilde has become both a symbol and a victim of the hypocrisy of his time.

And, also like Socrates, he has, in succumbing to the destructive forces of that hypocrisy, become a martyr for the truth.

I maintain that few artists, living or dead — John Irving, Whistler, or even George Bernard Shaw among them — could make a similar claim. | 143

* * *

My affection for Oscar Wilde is by now apparent. I don't doubt much of it stems from the manner I was first introduced to him and the way my opinion of him was suddenly changed by my involvement with this small-town amateur production of his work.

As I had guessed, I was cast as Jack Worthing. This was my first onstage role, and I spent the next three months of my life both learning how to act and learning a new appreciation for the playwright. Rehearsals were held every Saturday and Sunday, while the theatre, which also doubled as our town's only cinema, was dark. I had little experience with theatre in those days, and I found myself completely charmed and fascinated by the whole encounter.

My first real love of it was based on the fact that there are no windows in a theatre, and so it is always dark and artificially lit. For someone who is what my mother always refers to as a "night owl," this was a relief. There was a sense of safety in being in a dark theatre, rehearsing all day, that I liked, a sense of being protected, being special, exempt from the ordinary rules of evolutionary survival that governed the rest of the world. We were creating art! We were actors! We were fashioning entertainments! There was, of course, a certain amount of pretension in all of this. We were not getting paid for our efforts, and most of us did have "real" jobs. Vernon was a schoolteacher. David worked at the Post Office. Susan, playing the part of Gwendolen, managed her father's inn. Brenda, the director, and Karen, who played Miss Prism, and my sister, who played Cecily, were all housewives. The formidable Lady Bracknell, in real life the formidable Susan Smith, worked at an insurance agency.

Stephen and I were the only real bums among the lot, as we both lived at home and called ourselves students.

But still, the production was an invaluable lesson for me. I learned the language of the theatre, which I find so delectable even today—blocking, scrims, upstage, downstage, greenroom, juliets, proscenium arches, front-of-house, bastard prompt, fifth business. I learned the basics of set design, and that most indispensable technique for performing modern drama: understatement. John, the theatre manager, designed all the sets for the plays, and he was brilliant. A tall tryptch, stage left, with hinged walls transformed in seconds from an indoor London drawing-room to an outdoor country English garden, and then to a manor library. The subtleties of lighting turned night to day, morning to afternoon, summer to fall. I learned, what seems to me now from this distance of time and experience the most obvious of theatrical lessons — never to let my expression slacken, even if I was not the one speaking, to analyze and catalogue my movements during the action of real life so I could reproduce them naturally while on stage.

To project.

Always to have one eye visible to the audience, even if the action called for me to be turned away.

Not to step out of my light, and, perhaps most importantly, as far as the other actors were concerned, never to upstage.

I managed most of these lessons well, though it seems to me now I was wooden and stilted in my performance. Then again, so was Jack Worthing in his demeanour, and so I may have been typecast after all.

But Stephen. Stephen was a revelation. Difficult and demaning backstage, on stage he *was* Algernon Moncrieff. His timing was perfect. (I still remember the absolute relish with which he ate each of Lady Bracknells' cucumber sandwiches on opening night, as if, dear God, he were actually enjoying them.) He was, like the play's creator, witty, urbane, intelligent, and utterly charming. He brought the house down with each performance.

At night, when we were out of the theatre, things were different.

Stephen and I had taken a shine to each other right away, for many reasons. Both of us were dying to escape the small, provincial backwater into which we had somehow, mistakenly, been born. Both of us had artistic ambitions (I wanted to be a writer, Stephen an actor). We liked to read, and to think aloud, and we considered ourselves budding intellectuals. We ate Chinese food at the town's only Chinese-food restaurant (Stephen insisted on referring to it, for some reason, as Cantonese) and discussed the philosophy of Plato and Hegel and Nietzsche, which we knew precious little about. The intellectual insouciance that Stephen projected when I first met him was just that: a projection. Underneath were as many insecurities and fears and self-perceived inadequacies as you'd care to count, and beneath that, the arrogance re-emerged, only smaller, harder, more scarred and less expansive, born out of the necessity of self-protection rather than any genuine belief that he was better than anyone else.

In other words, as I suspected that very first day I met him, Stephen was — like me, like Oscar Wilde and possibly even Vernon, the sweet and airy Reverend Chasuble — a homosexual.

II

I visited Oscar Wilde's grave on my very first visit to Paris in the autumn of 1998. Wilde is buried in Père Lachaise cemetery in the twentieth arrondissement, amid such Paris literati as Gertrude Stein, Molière, Balzac, Marcel Proust, Colette and many others. The cemetery is most well known for housing the grave of the sixties rock star Jim Morrison, who died of a drug overdose in the city in 1972 when he was twenty-eight. Hordes of dope-smoking, tie-dyed, latter-day hippy types visit the grave each year, and toss beer bottles and marijuana roaches and cigarette butts on the grave in some kind of perverse homage, while a security guard stands by to make sure no one commits any more serious vandalism. (Morrison's is the only grave with its own, twenty-four-hour security.)

It used to be the policy of the city, and perhaps still is, that anyone who died within the gates of Paris could be buried in Père Lachaise for free, which explains why so many of the world's famous ended up there, among a much larger contingent of wealthy unknowns. In order to make room for the many thousands who died within the gates of Paris each year (and whose families all wanted them buried at such a prestigious address and among such distinguished company), the policy was that if your grave was not visited in a period of two years your body would be disinterred and buried outside the gates in a less well-known cemetery. This gave way to the practice, in the late nineteenth and early twentieth centuries, of the hiring of official "grave-sitters" — persons who would visit the graves of the loved ones of wealthy families who couldn't find time themselves but also didn't want their relatives disinterred.

| 147

Wilde's grave, like Morrison's and a few of the other more famous residents of Père Lachaise, has no need for an official grave-sitter. Next to Morrison's, Wilde's grave is the most frequented in the cemetery, which is saying something, when buried next to the likes of composer Frédéric Chopin and the French Impressionist painter Camille Pissarro.

Wilde died in complete poverty in 1900, and was first buried in the less well-known Bagneaux cemetery, though from the start there were plans to bury him in Père Lachaise. He was buried in "quicktime" — a process that allows the body to be interred in an unsealed casket so when the time comes for transfer the process can be done cleanly, without flesh and other organic matter. He was moved to Père Lachaise on July 19, 1909. The tomb that houses his remains today was sculpted by the American artist Jacob Epstein; when it was unveiled, featuring the anatomically correct figure of an Egyptian male, the cemetery conservator judged it indecent. A fig leaf was fashioned to cover the more blatant anatomy, but in 1922 students from the University of Paris hacked away the leaf, and removed a portion of the figure's sculpted penis in the process — an irony that only Wilde himself could have commented on with the wit and energy it deserves.

The grave was an impressive sight the day I first visited it, a wet and dreary morning in October. The granite of the tomb was marked, as it has been on all subsequent visits, with lipstick kisses, which I suspect is the work of legions of drag queens making a pilgrimage, or perhaps there is just one Parisian drag queen, who has made this his/her life's work. There are letters, some also written in lipstick and others in ink, scribbled hastily on scraps of paper and placed on the base of the tomb, held down against marauding winds by small stones picked off the ground. I left my own note that day, which I shall keep private, and copied down the inscription on the tomb from Wilde's own *Ballad of Reading Gaol*: "And alien tears will fill for him / Pities long broken urn. / For his mourners will be outcast men / And outcasts always mourn." I have not been so profoundly affected by a grave, either before or since, and I can only surmise it is because the tomb of this man stands as a symbol for what we have all felt, growing up outcast in a rigid, unforgiving society. For those of us who are brave enough, we have, like Wilde, taken what was a secret and made it public, and felt humiliation and shame and been cast out because of it.

Wilde's grave stands for more than coming out of the closet. It is also a symbol of his final triumph. Here we are, a hundred years later, and men and woman visit it in droves, kiss it, publicly announce their gratitude to him for his symbolic importance. Before Wilde, homosexuality was not discussed, except in works of Greek literature and philosophy (which were tolerated because of their age and intellectual remoteness). Wilde changed all that. After his famous trials, homosexuality would become a public debate in the West that continues to this day. (As I write this the case for gay marriage is still being fiercely debated among politicians in the United States.) In the gay villages of the larger of our cities, his namesake is everywhere — on restaurants, bookstores, bars, magazines, festivals, streets. He is still being talked about in books and essays such as these. Like Socrates and Jesus Christ, the establishment, by persecuting him, would make him stronger and more powerful in death than he ever was in life. He stands tall now even among the legendary figures of the nineteenth century — as a writer, thinker, social commentator, and, most of all, as the symbolic father of gay liberation. His infamous trial was not just about being homosexual, but was, as I see it now from this comfortable distance of time and place and perspective, the beginning of gay.

* * *

My own beginning of gay, as I now see it but didn't then, was during that production of Wilde's play. It was the first time I seriously gave thought to becoming a writer, and the two are entirely related in my mind.

I had written before then, and I always knew I was gay. Both were essentially secret activities, though one was more secret than the other. During that production, for the first time, I connected the *act* of writing with the act of *producing* what I wrote for public consumption. I started writing plays, with the idea that this troupe would one day, and not very far off either, begin producing them (which they did). At the same time, Stephen and I were becoming closer, and I realized that behind the facade of intellectual companionship lurked something deeper, more imperative, more primal. I began to look forward to rehearsals more as a way of spending time with Stephen than of running my lines. This desire was not exactly unrequited. It seemed Stephen would rather spend his evenings with me in the restaurant, or the café, or in the back of the theatre while everyone else was in the lobby getting ready to go home.

I had gay sex for the first time that summer. Not with Stephen, but with an older man from my village. We got drunk at a party together, and ended up in his car at the end of a long dirt road beside a lake in the middle of the night. I wasn't in love with him or even particularly attracted to him. But I was young, intoxicated, horny, naive. Like generations of teenagers before me, both gay and straight, I lost my virginity in the cramped backseat of a car with the stereo thumping out the insistent rhythms of the day.

A few weeks later Stephen and I were in his parents' car by the ocean, and this time I was sober. I had taken my shoes off, and Stephen suggested I stretch them across his lap and "get comfortable." We talked, as he lightly rubbed his hand up and down my naked shin (I was wearing shorts) and I thought this would be it, finally I was going to have sex with someone I loved.

It didn't happen. I'm not sure what happened in its place. I believed then, and still believe, that Stephen felt at least *some* of what I did — that the charged sexual and emotional atmosphere in that car did not come from my imagination alone. Perhaps he chickened out, or didn't feel as strongly for me as I did for him. Whatever the reason, Stephen suggested we leave because we had dress rehearsal the next day, and a half-hour later he dropped me off at my aunt's house, where I was staying for the night.

Dress rehearsal was a catastrophe (which is a good thing in the theatre) and opening night went well. On the surface, my relationship with Stephen remained the same, and we still went for coffee and Chinese food, still discussed philosophy and theatre, novels and music. At the end of the summer, I met my first boyfriend on a weekend trip to Halifax and Stephen started preparing to go to Montreal for school. We grew apart. The next I heard of him, he'd had a nervous breakdown in his brother's apartment in Montreal. He was shipped back to Liverpool to convalesce at his parents' house, and I never heard another word from him. | 151

III

I often think about Stephen and wonder what he is doing. As far as I know, he never once stood up and announced to the world he was gay; it is not for me to make that announcement for him, and so I will at least *concede* the possibility that he is not.) I ran into his younger brother in a bar in Montreal years later; he *is* openly gay and was studying to be a doctor. I asked him about Stephen, but he was evasive in his answers, saying that he was still in Liverpool. As far as I know, Stephen never accomplished any of those things we talked about so passionately — writing, acting, singing, becoming an artist. What else did or didn't he accomplish? Is he married? What does he do for a living? Does he still read philosophy and eat Chinese food? Does he have children? Is his hair as blonde and are his eyes as blue as I remember them? Does he still walk into a room as if he has been there a million times before and knows its every nook and cranny, and the people in it, even if he has never stepped foot in it before and those it contains are strangers? Does he love someone? Does he love himself?

Is he, for God's sake, even still alive?

All our pasts, of course, are littered with such figures. For every one of us who achieves at least some semblance of our dreams and becomes what we set out to become, there are many around us who do not. For every Oscar there are a thousand Lord Alfred Douglases. At a recent reading in Nova Scotia, I was asked if I would write a new play for the Winds of Change theatre troupe and the International Theatre Festival they now hold in Liverpool every two years. I agreed, but it never worked out. Any play written for the festival must be largely visual, due to the international nature of the audience. For awhile, I dreamed of returning for one summer to that theatre where somehow everything that I have become, the good and the bad and the indefinable, was set in motion. In some of my more romantic moments, a certain blonde-haired, anaemic, but still handsome middle-aged man wanders laconically into the theatre to try out. And no matter what part he auditioned for in my play, my long-lost friend would have been instantly cast.

MOISE AND
THE WORLD OF
TENNESSEE WILLIAMS

In July of 2003, I was asked to read during Gay
Pride Week in Halifax, Nova Scotia at an annual literary festival
called Reading Out Loud. A strange and refreshing take on the
usual queer reading festival, the one-night affair asks authors and
local gay celebrities to read not from their own works but from the
writings of their favourite gay and lesbian authors, something that
for them has meaning and fits into their own personal canon of
gay literature.

As usual, I was in a rush when I left my apartment in Toronto
to catch the plane for Halifax for that portion of my book tour,
and I forgot the book I was planning to read from: the much
overlooked one and only novel by perhaps the best American
playwright, Tennessee Williams.

Had it been practically any other novel, I would have bought
another copy in Halifax and read from it, or borrowed one from
the library (the event was located at the Spring Garden branch of
the Halifax Public Library), but, alas, as I knew from previous
experience, not only was *Moise and the World of Reason* out of print,
it was almost impossible to get. First editions were always available

from rare and used bookstores on the Internet, but I had eight hours, not three weeks, to get my hands on a copy. I couldn't wait for the usual slow paced Internet delivery.

So I chose the second of my favourite gay classic novels, James Baldwin's *Giovanni's Room*, to read from instead. And though *Giovanni's Room* is a great book, and nearly as dear to my heart as Williams' (not to mention being available from practically any bookstore or library in the world), *Moise* will always be my favourite. And if not as influential as Baldwin's book, it is only because those who now shape the Williams' canon nearly always leave it out.

* * *

Some would argue that the reason *Moise* is left out of the Williams' canon is that it is not a great book. Williams was, after all, a playwright, and some of his prose pieces (I am thinking particularly of his short stories, such as "Field of Blue Children") are perfect examples of writing celebrated for the fame of the author rather than any intrinsic literary value. His short stories are overwritten, in my opinion; the language is often florid with so many inexact qualifiers that it annoys the hell out of me by the second page. But not only does *Moise* avoid the self-indulgent trap of these short stories, it transcends, in some ways, even the brilliance of the plays. The writing is fresh, vigorous, and, for its time, innovative. The dialogue is some of the snappiest I've ever read; the characters so clearly drawn that they hang in my memory, eerily distinct, some ten years after first reading the novel.

Like the decade it was written in, *Moise* is a complicated story. It is narrated by a nameless gay man from Thelma, Alabama living in Manhattan, whose best friend, Moise (pronounced Moy-Ease), an underground legend and poverty-stricken painter, has invited all her friends and enemies and casual acquaintances to her basement flat in Manhattan to announce her "retirement" from the world of reason.

Moise is a character resonant of many of the young women I used to know from my Halifax university days — a formidable mass of intellectual and emotional contradiction: wan and pretty, brilliant and unmotivated, intelligent and bored, talented and undisciplined. The novel chronicles one night in Greenwich Village and deals with the quadrangular relationship between the anonymous narrator and his lover, Charlie, Moise, and the narrator's remembrances of his dead lover Lance, an African American figure skater — the self-proclaimed "nigger on ice." The narrator struggles between the recalled innocence of his Southern childhood, the naiveté of his relationship with the figure skater, and his present state — a gradual submersion into the seedy sexual subculture of New York and his friendship with a famous but morally derelict author (clearly based on Williams himself).

Williams' style is experimental: the narrator sometimes ends chapters in mid sentence, or stops in the middle of a paragraph to give us an unrelated stream of consciousness. But it is also absolutely typical of its period in portraying the advent of the individual's alienation from Western society, exacerbated by the decay of the moral and social fabric of urban America. In a way he never did in his plays, Williams graphically describes sexual congress in this book, bringing his considerable powers of description to bear on anal sex and fellatio, among other practices, in passages that are, rare enough for any literature — gay or straight — both erotic and beautifully written. For this reason alone, the novel deserves more play than it has ever received from the guardians of the gay literary canon.

* * *

Like every other literate gay man I know, I went through my love affair with Williams' plays in my teenage years, when, like the plays themselves, I always bordered on sexual revelation without actually ever achieving it. Later, from a political standpoint, I became disillusioned with Williams' work, as it seemed to me he never truly dealt with the obvious homosexual concerns in his plays, except indirectly. The closest he ever came was with Sebastian in *Suddenly Last Summer*, who never appears in the play except through the dialogue of the characters; or with Brick, who remembers an unconsummated love affair with his dead best friend as he's lying in bed with a broken leg in his family's mansion in the American South. In *Moise*, Williams comes out of the closet with full force. The novel is as gay, and as graphic, as any piece of literature can be, and, likely for this very reason, has been dismissed by the largely heterosexual promoters of Williams' work.

But it is odd that the gay community has never picked up on the book. Perhaps it is because the world of *Moise* is so unremittingly bleak; the characters neither affirm nor deny the inherent "rightness" of their sexuality. The book ends with Moise and the narrator seducing a telephone installer, as Moise bends him over for the narrator to penetrate him, providing what I think may be one of the most memorable endings to any novel I have ever read.

Giovanni's Room is likewise bleak in its portrayal of the young lovers David and Giovanni, ending in tragedy when David chooses a life of heterosexuality in the United States and abandons his lover in a small room on the outskirts of Paris. I suspect that the Baldwin book is more enduringly popular because it offers, at least, a clear-cut moral choice. Be gay and in love, and live a poor but passionate existence, or deny yourself and live a straight, socially acceptable but hollow life. *Giovanni's Room* was one of the first books of its kind to offer us this choice, and condemned the characters because they didn't follow their own homosexual nature. (The trend prior to Baldwin, at least with straight writers portraying gay characters, was to do the opposite — condemn gay characters if they "gave in" to their tendencies.) But Williams' novel ends in a sort of moral impasse, with the narrator affirming his sexuality on the one hand and giving in to his own self-loathing on the other by engaging in an endless string of compulsive, same-sex physical encounters that are, ultimately, meaningless and self-defeating and devoid of any kind of lasting value. As for many of us, the narrator's early naiveté and innocence is obliterated, but his sense of shame at being different is not. He accepts his homosexuality on a purely physical level, and in the place of true self-acceptance offers himself simple diversion and repeated sexual conquest. For a good number of gay men, this author included, who spend far too many hours hunting the streets and parks and bathhouses and bars for meaningless, anonymous compulsive encounters of our own, Williams' book hits a little too close to home. This may explain its being so often overlooked in favour of Baldwin and other gay authors of the period. Perhaps one day, when the dust has settled, it will be restored to its rightful place at or near the top of the canon of classic gay literature.

OUR
BELOVED PARIS

Most people go to Paris to fall in love. I fell out of it. Three o'clock in the morning and my lover and I were standing in the centre of the rue d'Austerlitz, shouting at each other in voices that echoed off the tall, narrow shafts of the buildings around us, until some old man hollered "Silence!" from his fourth-storey window in what was likely the only English he knew besides hello and goodbye, please and thank you.

Hello and goodbye.

David threatened to leave that night, to sleep in the car, and catch a train for London from the Gare de Lyon and then a plane from Heathrow back to Canada. I convinced him to stay, though we slept in separate beds (our room, as usual when a gay couple ask for a room anywhere in the world, came with two singles instead of one double). Our conversation over breakfast on the rue Diderot the next morning was calmer, but underneath it I felt the usual remnants of a failed relationship — sadness, anger, violence, hurt, resentment, accusation.

From that moment, despite the lies we told ourselves and the nearly three weeks we spent together after that, roaming around the narrow, teeming streets of Europe's ancient cities, we both knew that it was over.

There were many nights in Paris after that night that I awoke in our *pension* on the d'Austerlitz thinking of home. Not of Ottawa and the one-bedroom apartment on Bronson Street that I had lived in for the past five years. No, I woke up dreaming of Greenfield, where I was raised. There were times, in those long, lonely days when David and I were bickering, where I would wake up in the middle of the night with the sound of the river in my ears, and the smell of fresh-cut grass and damp pine needles in my nose. I would be so sick with longing and nostalgia that it would be hours before I could fall back asleep. In the morning, I would try to capture in my journal the essence of these dreams and feelings. I would sit down at the *brasserie* on the nearest boulevard over café with crème trying to act like some latter-day Hemingway.

It never worked.

I'd discovered years before on other visits that Paris, despite its reputation, is not conducive to good writing. At least not for me. Maybe it's because so much of note has already been written there that in the back of my mind as I try to work is the thought, "What could I possibly add to it?" Or sometimes I think it's simply because a lot of people come to Paris hoping to be inspired, and what we are instead is horrified at the cost of everything; at the dog turds drying on the sidewalks; at how rude people can be; at how a relationship that once seemed to be all you wanted in the world can suddenly go bad and you find yourself alone in a flea-infested hotel you can barely afford.

But I tried anyway.

I was a great believer, and sometimes still am, in the idea that all art is forged in adversity.

Too bad I'd never heard that one about knowing when to quit. | 161

III

It was David's first time in Paris, and he had not really liked it as much as he thought he would. He had been disappointed in the hard layer of reality under the frosting of romantic popular perception, and he never had time to discover the other Paris, that of quiet side streets and local *brasseries*, away from the touristy bustle of the Champs Elysées and the Eiffel Tower and Sacre-Coeur. I tried to show him this. I took him to Père Lachaise to see the graves of Gertrude Stein, Oscar Wilde, Chopin, and Proust.

"Big deal," he complained. 'Dead people and a bunch of rocks."

I took him to Montparnasse, the Marais, the Parc de Villete, the Tuileries Gardens, the smaller, less well-known open-air markets, and the book and art dealers on the Quai d'Orsay on Saturday and Sunday. He remained spectacularly unimpressed by all of it. Because we were there in the summer, there was very little music worth listening to; the Paris Opera and Opera Bastille were closed in July and August and most of the performances listed in *Paris Voice* were concerts held in churches to ensnare tourists: two hundred francs to hear some hastily assembled amateur quintet in period costume butcher Vivaldi or Chopin.

David, who played classical piano, composed music, and had studied at the music conservatory in Vancouver, complained that most of the tourists were too stupid to notice, and Parisians couldn't care less. "One thousand years of musical tradition," he said, "and everyone here listens to Madonna and Celine Dion."

162| And after only a week or so, we left the City of Light for the Concertgebow in Amsterdam; and then it was back to Spain, where we caught a boat from Bilbao to Portsmouth, from where we went on to London, the final city on our itinerary. I was okay with leaving Paris. In the times I'd been to the city before, I'd been single, and was free to enjoy all the things about the city I loved. I'd always stayed in the twelfth arrondissement. The hotels along the rue d'Austerlitz are some of the cheapest in the city, the restaurants are good, and it is not overrun with American tourists, who prefer the more upscale eleventh, first or even the fifteenth near the Eiffel Tower. I'd also chosen it, in the years I'd first started coming to France, before I met David, for its relative proximity to the Marais, and the restaurants and sex clubs and gay bars there. The summer before I'd picked up a twenty-year-old blonde French boy whose skin was as soft as a girl's. I fucked him in the single bed, and in the morning pretended to be asleep when he got up and dressed and softly left the hotel room. When I came down for breakfast the manager at the front desk stopped me and asked if I would pay for the extra guest in my room for the night.

"But he was only there for a few hours," I said. "And you didn't say anything about guests when I checked in."

"Yes," he replied in French," but I'm telling you now. It's thirty euros."

"Where is it written that I can't have guests?" I asked.

"It's not written but it's still policy," he said. I could discern a vague distaste that had nothing to do with money, but asking for money was the only way he could safely express it. Or maybe I was reading too much into it. After all, separating Americans from their dollar has become the national sport of France. It didn't matter that I was from Canada and not the United States; to most Europeans the difference is nominal. I argued for a few more minutes and then gave in; I handed over the extra thirty euros "for my guest" and swore that next time I would just hire myself a prostitute and be done with it. An hour later I found myself at my usual sidewalk table on the corner of rue d'Austerlitz and boulevard Diderot, scribbling furiously in my journal, drinking coffee and smoking cigarette after cigarette, huddled under the awning to protect myself from the ubiquitous Paris rain.

IV

I have always had a knack for fitting in, but have never mastered the art of belonging. In Paris, tourists always stop me on the street to ask directions. Parisians take one look at me and know that I am from away. Yet, in this strange limbo between visitor and native, I can exist without being overly bothered by anyone. The first time I visited the city was in May of 1998. Like David, I expected more from her. I arrived on a bus from Dover at six in the morning and spent the day wandering around the streets near my hotel in the fifteenth arrondissement. I had always been a fan of the expatriate writers — Hemingway, Fitzgerald, Joyce, and Dorothy Parker — and it was this intellectual, bohemian spirit I was looking for when I strolled Montparnasse, poking my head into cafés, half expecting to see famous writers that had been dead for fifty years sitting at tables scribbling into their notebooks, black coffee laced with brandy at the ready.

I didn't find them. I found instead a city much like the cities I had known back home — studded with coffee shops and McDonald's restaurants and department stores and the usual urban blight of modern-day franchise consumerism. Except for admittedly glorious architecture, most of which was overrun with American tourists, Paris was a huge disappointment. I eventually moved from the student hostel in the fifteenth to the rue d'Austerlitz in the twelfth on the other side of the river, and there began spending my mornings in the cafés, working furiously on my second novel. The novel wasn't going very well (I would eventually, in Istanbul of all places, give it up and wait for a better idea to come along), but at this stage I was still full of hope for it. I sat under the awning of the nearest *brasserie* writing and drinking my café every day, as if the mere act of working would somehow make this story start to flow. I was rarely approached as I hunched over my notebook, except by the occasional desperate prostitute working the early-morning shift on the Diderot, or someone asking for a cigarette.

These were the days when I did not worry about my smoking. I enjoyed it. Not like those last few years before I quit, when each cigarette brought with it ten minutes of obsession over the possibility of lung cancer and hard, long, resentful stares from my fascist non-smoking neighbours at the nearest table, of which Canada seemed to have a disproportionately large number. But there was none of this in Paris. Paris is a smoker's city, or at least it was then. You could smoke on the subway, the bus, even atop the Eiffel Tower. If you asked for a non-smoking table at a restaurant, they sent you to Switzerland.

I smoked unfiltered Gitanes, because they were French-made | 165
and bland Canadian cigarettes weren't available and I was ahead of my time in eschewing anything American for political reasons (Coca Cola, Marlboros, McDonald's, Starbucks). By the time David and I came to Paris I had quit smoking. After we fought, I started again for a brief period. I also started going out to the same café alone in the morning and writing. On my second day at the café with my journal, with David back at the *pension*, I was on my fifth cigarette of the morning and my second coffee when a yellow taxicab came screeching to a halt on the street in front of me, startling me so I jerked my hand into my coffee cup, spilled some on my papers and burnt myself.

"Fuck!" I cried loudly in English, but all was lost in the ensuing chaos. A pretty young woman and the driver jumped out of the car at the same time, screaming at each other. The woman was French; the cabbie Middle Eastern. He was young, and incredibly handsome. "You pig," said the woman in English. "You filthy swine. You ridiculous peacock of a man."

"You were nothing more than a whore when I found you," the man replied. "You're still a whore, without a clientele."

"Baise-toi," said the woman.

"La même chose à toi," replied the cabbie.

The French have some of the most expressive curses in the world. What makes it even more interesting, to an Anglo at least, is how beautifully and effortlessly they roll off the tongue — unlike the harsh, guttural sounds of their English counterparts, French curses sound cleaner and more poetic than they really are. And these two people, standing in the middle of street around the stalled cabbie shouting at each other, were speaking some of the most impressively fluent filth I had ever heard; apparently, I was not the only one who thought so. The entire population of the *brasserie* had turned out onto the patio to huddle under the awning out of the rain and see what was going on, including the waiters in their stiff white aprons, with their arms crossed over their broad chests, smiling and nodding at each other at the scene in front of them.

"Putain," I heard one whisper knowingly behind me.

Finally, the woman turned away from the cabbie, and started into the café. Leaving his door open he ran around the front of the car and grabbed her roughly by the arm.

"You owe me money," he said to her. "You can't go anywhere."

"I can go anywhere I want!" she said defiantly. "You don't own me."

"Everyone owns you. You're cheap. We can all afford it! Even the poorest of us!"

A few unkind laughs came from some of the men standing around on the patio and on the sidewalk. The woman glared at them and tried to pull herself haughtily away from the driver's grip; the cabbie, emboldened by the sudden encouragement, shook her harder.

"Where is my money?" he shouted. "You give me all my money."
"Terroriste," cried the woman finally. "Je pourrais vous dire des choses au sujet de ce qu'il est. Terroriste!"
The cabbie blanched and let her go. This time no one laughed, and the woman, straightening her blouse, looked at him and, amazingly, stuck out her tongue. "Go back to Algeria," she said suddenly in English. The faces of those standing around were not so amused; they saw him now as a foreigner. He realized this, and | 167 started to back away towards his cab.
"I'll find you," he whispered "I'll get what is mine."
"You'll get the clap," said the woman, seemingly almost completely recovered from the confrontation by now. I hadn't moved from my table next to the sidewalk, and so I had the closest view of all the action. When the woman came onto the patio, away from the driver, she was standing right next to me. She looked down, and said, "Avez-vous une cigarette?"
I opened my pack, gave her one, and to my surprise she sat down at my table and lit it with my lighter. The cabbie glared at me from over the top of his cab before he got back into it. He drove off, squealing his tires. The bystanders began to drift away and back inside the café. The woman smiled at me, as if we had just met under normal circumstances.
"Vous êtes américain, oui?"
"Canadien," I answered.
"Québécois?"
"Ontario."
"Vous visitez Paris? Pourquoi?"
"Pour me détendre."

The woman laughed harshly, barking smoke out of her nostrils. She switched suddenly to English.

"Relax in Paris? There are better places to relax, yes?"

"You speak English."

She shrugged. "I learned, yes. Long ago. I thought once of moving to New York."

"Why didn't you?"

"L'argent est bas."

"I see."

The waiters and the customers had all gone back inside by now. The only customers on the patio were myself, the woman, and a middle-aged man with blow-dried, obviously bleached-blonde hair, sitting to the left of us with a white poodle perched on his lap. It had stopped raining. The woman watched the man as she lit her cigarette. He was feeding his dog scraps of bacon from his plate.

"Tapette," the woman said.

"I should go," I told her.

"What is your name?" she asked, as if she hadn't heard me.

"Darren."

"A strange name."

"I was named after a cousin of mine."

"And you're English. It's odd that you smoke. Most *anglais* don't smoke."

"Really?" I said, growing uninterested. "I really should be going. It was nice meeting you."

"Don't go," she said, and reached across and touched the top of my hand. Lightly. Pleadingly. I looked into the woman's eyes and realized, despite the brassy blonde hair and the makeup, that she was even younger than I had first thought. Twenty-five perhaps.

Maybe less. Yet she looked tired, haggard. I realized she didn't have a coat, and the air was chilly, even for Paris in July. It would probably rain again.

"The man," I said. "He was really a terrorist?"

She sat back, dragged on the cigarette, considered me.

"No. He is just a cab driver."

"He is your lover?"

"Was my lover. Now I suspect he would like to kill me."

"What did you do?"

"I rejected him."

Just then the waiter came and, as stiff as his apron, asked if I would like anything else. He wouldn't even look at the woman. I made a point of asking her if she wanted something.

"Un café," she said.

"Avec crème?" I asked her.

"Oui," she said.

The waiter nodded. "The Algerian," she said, after the waiter had left. "He asked me to marry him. And I said no. That's why he hates me now."

"Why did you say no?"

"Because he is Muslim. He wants me to wear a burka and scrub his toilets and give him a dozen children."

"And he is not a terrorist?"

She crushed her cigarette in the ashtray and shook her head. "He is afraid everyone will think he is. It is very difficult for Middle Eastern men in Paris right now. Everyone is afraid, and suspicious."

"Are you a prostitute?"

The question was out of my mouth before I had time to stop it. The woman only smiled slightly and shook her head, looked away from me at the man still feeding and making a fuss over his dog.

"No," she said. "He is not a terrorist. I am not a whore."

She said this in French, and it struck me, for some reason, as being peculiarly resonant; for long afterwards, I would remember this phrase from the nameless woman, spoken quietly and succinctly in her own language.

Il n'est pas un terroriste. Je ne suis pas une putain.

V

I spent my afternoons that summer in the galleries of Paris. Paris has more art galleries per capita than any other city in Europe. Besides big ones — like the Louvre and the Musée d'Orsay, the Musée Picasso, and the Galerie Nationale — there were all kinds of smaller, interesting, out-of-the-way galleries and collections that are inexpensive to visit. Some of them, like the reopened Kahnweiler gallery in the ninth arrondisement, are famous in their own right.

This had been the one passion David and I had shared: art. The two of us spent all our days in Europe that summer prowling the galleries. We didn't discriminate. We might spend the morning at a once private collection, now opened up to the public in an old converted mansion off the Champs Elysées, viewing obscure Canalettos and Turners and works by Pieter Brueghel the Younger, and the afternoon at a special exhibit of Jean Cocteau or Louise Bourgeois or Marcel Duchamp at the Pompidou. We loved to discuss art, to conceptualize, to theorize, to compare.

For both of us, our artistic lineage was somewhat convoluted. David was adopted, and came from a working-class family in rural Manitoba. For a long while the only art I knew was the paint-by-numbers landscapes that hung above the sofa in the living room back home that had been rendered lovingly if inexpertly by a favourite aunt. Surprisingly, my father gave me a book on Impressionist painters for Christmas when I was fifteen. My father didn't know I was interested in art (he couldn't know it, for I didn't even | 171 know it myself yet), but he had waited until the last minute, as usual, to do his shopping and had thoughtlessly picked it up from a bookstore in the nearest town (Greenfield didn't have a grocery store, let alone a bookstore) because it was in the remainders bin. Its price had been reduced by 75 per cent.

I was hooked. All Christmas day I pored over the volume, looking at the reproductions of famous paintings that I had never heard of. It was filled with what I now know to be the usual representatives from that period — Monet, Manet, Renoir, Degas, Pissarro, Caillebotte, Cassatt, Cézanne, Toulouse-Lautrec. For the first time, I was struck by the spiritual intensity of a painting as well as the artist's ability to reproduce what he or she was looking at. My eye was drawn to certain things — the dashed-off blobs of colour meant to represent poppies in Monet's *Fields in Spring*. The corsage on the prostitute/bartender and the glittering champagne bottles in Manet's *Bar at the Folies-Bergère*. The paintings were both gloriously indistinct and remarkably accurate in the way they reproduced certain sensations, certain *impressions*, of light and shadow, without the painstaking detail of what that light and shadow was falling upon or against.

Although I didn't know it then, what I was looking at was the first stirrings of modernism in the world, just as I was feeling the first stirrings of a passion for visual art within myself. For a while afterwards, I wanted to be an artist, though I quickly found out I had no particular talent for it. I was content then to simply study art, in what books I could get from my school library or the bookmobile that came into our village every Thursday evening from seven to eight, and, later, to write about it. I was careful to keep this new-found hobby a secret from nearly everyone, including my father. He had given me the book, because he knew that I liked to read, but he had hardly done more than glance at the title. If he had known how much time I spent looking through books about art, he would have likely thought it strange.

As it was, I always felt emanating from him some slight disapproval that he had never quite dared put into words. He wasn't a cruel or a mean man. He rarely hit me, or made fun of me, or called me names. He could be surprisingly compassionate and kind about some things, like the summer he came home with brand new bicycles for my brother, sister, and me, and the way he'd always take us shopping on Saturday mornings, where he would always break down and buy us some small thing if we pestered him enough.

But, at the same time, he was a masculine man, who believed in sports, and sweat, and competition, and I don't think he could help but notice he wasn't raising the most masculine of sons. I was terrible at most sports. I first disappointed him, at a young age, when I failed to play hockey. I couldn't stand up on the skates properly. I was (and am) ambidextrous when it comes to guns and hockey sticks, and so could never decide in which hand I wanted to hold the stick (I had the same problem with the brush when I tried to paint years later). On skates, I kept falling down, and if I didn't I was an easy mark for kids at public skate who wanted to hone their cross-checking skills. At school, during gym class, I was the "master of disaster," as one high-school wit put it. On the basketball court, the other boys would make fun of me for dropping the ball, and never, to my recollection, completing a lay-up. Once I was slammed so hard up against the wall by an older boy in the hallway to the gym that my collarbone was snapped cleanly in two. I fell to the floor screaming and writhing in agony, and the other boys ran out. The man that passed by — an industrial arts teacher who had once made fun of me in front of the entire class of boys because I "laughed like a girl" — simply smiled and shook his head and walked on, as if he thought I was manufacturing my pain with my usual feminine flair for dramatics. At dinner, my right arm wrapped in a gauge sling and holding my fork awkwardly in my left, my father told me that I needed to fight back.

"He's got to learn to stand up to these bullies," he said to my mother. "They do it to him once, they'll do it to him every time."

"Can I go to bed now? I'm tired."

"If you stand up to them just once, even if they kick the shit out of you, they'll at least know they can't get away with it and they'll leave you alone."

Eventually, at my mother's urging, my father let me up from the table and I went to my room. I was excused from gym class for a month, because I was still in the sling, and even when the sling came off, no one mentioned sports to me again. A few years later, when I was nineteen and shortly after I met my first boyfriend, I told my father I was gay. It didn't go well. I also told my younger brother that night, when the two of us were lying in our separate beds in our shared bedroom after midnight, and trying to sleep despite the heat. My brother didn't respond.

"Did you hear what I said?" I asked him.

"I heard."

"Aren't you going to say anything?"

"What's to say? You are what you are. Nothing I say's gonna change that, is it?"

"No," I said, reluctant to have my news so easily dismissed but unable, as always, to get past my family's unsophisticated but sound use of logic. "I guess it isn't."

And so it had gone.

Always, at the Musée d'Orsay, or anywhere else I saw a painting by Monet or any of the artists in that book I had received from my father all those years ago, I thought of him, and my family, and Greenfield, and how far away from all of that I'd ended up. I was legend there now — the boy who had escaped, who had done something, had gone somewhere. Of course, when you are always reminded by everything of the place you come from, it should be easy enough to tell that you never really escape from it. As a friend said once when we were having a similar discussion about our respective pasts, we carry our prisons with us.